All About
METHOD
Acting

NED MANDERINO

Manderino Books
Los Angeles

.

A word of gratitude to "Chip" DuBose, Mary Hardy and
Anita Colby for their much appreciated help in preparing
this book. Thanks, also, to Alejandro Rey, Paul Smith and
Delos V. Smith, Jr.

This book is for all my students.

ISBN: 0-9601194-3-4
Library of Congress Catalog Card Number: 85-090358

Portions of this book previously published in THE TRANSPER-
SONAL ACTOR ©1976 by Ned Manderino.
Sixth Printing

Contents

IV CONTENTS

Part II Technique Exercises

Part III Combinations: A Wealth of Nuances

Appendix

Introduction

The Method and the Stanislavski System have been written about with wit by Robert Lewis and with dynamic language by Harold Clurman. *Strasberg at the Actors Studio* conveys the electrical chemistry of Lee Strasberg's personality. Edward Easty's book, *On Method Acting*, reveals his personal recollections of studies with Strasberg. Even though I have had many years of experience with the Method, I have refrained from including personal reminiscences in this book. My main wish is to clarify Method crosscurrents in a useful way for the actor. There are many Method anecdotes and stories which the interested reader can encounter in other publications. My aim is to present Method knowledge to you so that you can discover which elements of the technique suit *your* personality.

The appeal of Method acting stems from its ability to inspire greater individuality in an acting gift. Method technique has gained an international reputation for creating behavior in a dynamic and naturalistic way. The

Method requires that the actor give less emphasis to the verbal interpretation of a writer's work, focusing instead on giving clarity to the inner interpretation of the writer's intention. Through the use of actions and the development of a more sensitive sensory awareness, the experience of a character is internalized, and, simultaneously, elements are created which acknowledge the necessity of outer characterization. This book emphasizes a technique that encompasses both the inner and outer principles of Method acting.

The creative seed of the Stanislavski Method was planted in American acting over sixty years ago. It continues to have an impact in the present, and the future holds great promise for the development of its infinite possibilities. As contemporarily embraced, it is divided into many practices and has been written about from numerous points of view.

One of our foremost critics on American acting, Harold Clurman, perceived the Stanislavski Method as a technique and system for instilling humanity in an actor's art. He pointed out the numerous benefits that American actors, directors, and writers have derived from it. Clurman regarded Method technique as a way of shaping both the inner and outer elements of the actor's instrument, and thus achieving striking characterizations. He believed that Stanislavski's principles would always be evolving as each new generation applied them to create authentic acting emotions.

As the Method has been applied in America, innumerable controversies have arisen about the "true" interpretation of Stanislavski's principles. Representatives of the opposing schools have accused each other of distorting and misinterpreting the Method, viewing each other as malpractitioners of the system. The central point of the furor concerns the belief that some who practice the Method overemphasize the creation of truthful inner emotion without giving attention to the important outer aspects needed to create a character in a dramatic situation. Many people feel that the Method is misused when the actor works with personal emotional experience in a way that neglects the outer essence of the character.

In other words, they would argue that the character's theatrical truth should not be given short shrift by the choices the Method actor uses to create personal emotion.

Lee Strasberg's interpretation of the Method has been at the center of the Method controversies for decades, with every other leading American Stanislavski disciple unable to reconcile themselves with Strasberg's emphasis on the personal inner emotion of the actor. The controversies revolve around the importance that Strasberg began to give to affective memory work during the training program of the Group Theater in the 1930's. Disagreement among the actors and directors of the Group Theater created artistic divisions which exist to this day.

My own experience with this issue is based on six years of study with Strasberg in his private workshop and at the Actors Studio. Contrary to what is frequently proclaimed, I cannot honestly conclude that Strasberg's teaching was overloaded with the use of the affective memory exercise. Although Strasberg may have emphasized the affective memory exercise during the fifties, this was no longer the case by the time I studied with him in the 1960's. During this period, I saw it done only twice and both times, Strasberg was very much in control of the emotion that surfaced. While I studied with him, Strasberg was primarily concerned with the sensory technique exercises, which nearly all Method acting teachers deem essential to an actor's development. Strasberg taught a means of making the acting instrument come alive with a basis of organic truth. He did not emphasize actions (sometimes called intentions) as other Method teachers do, but neither did he dismiss actions as being unimportant. He never objected when I combined actions and sensory choices in the projects I did in the Actors Studio Directors Unit.

In my sixteen years of teaching Method principles, I have never had a student use an affective memory exercise because I feel that actors are able to achieve comparable or better results with other technique choices. Due to its historical significance, I have included the affective memory exercise in this book for those who might find it of value.

In addition to Strasberg and Clurman, the other prominent Stanislavski Method teachers who began their work in the 1930's are Stella Adler, Robert Lewis, Elia Kazan, Sanford Meisner, and Morris Carnovsky. These teachers specialized in different aspects of the Method. When the Actors Studio was formed in 1947, Kazan taught technique exercises involving sensory recall, while Lewis taught the use of actions or intentions. When they later worked together to form an instructional approach for the Lincoln Center Training Program, Kazan asked Lewis to focus his concentration on intentions and style and to not dwell on emotional recall.

In his teaching, Lewis emphasizes the need for an actor's internal work to be seen externally. For him, an actor is an artist when transformation occurs. But even Lewis, the supreme stylist among the Stanislavski Method directors, underscored the usefulness of sensory training when he formed a program of acting at Yale University. He feels that an actor's work can lack a sense of truth without sensory training. Lewis's autobiography, *Slings and Arrows*, contains numerous photographs in which we see him in various disguises achieved with makeup and costume. Clearly, outer elements with an inner basis have always permeated his work as an actor, director, and teacher.

Along with Method technique training, I have always given attention to the actor's speech and movement as tools for outer expression. Many actors who study with me have already had training in other disciplines that contribute to the external expression of an actor's work, such as speech, movement, makeup, costume and scene design, as well as fencing, Yoga, and T'ai Chi. The goal of such actors during Method training is to refine and deepen the fusion of the inner and outer expression.

While the conflicts over interpretations of the Method have had unfortunate repercussions, they have served an important purpose by illustrating that the Method is an evolving technique. Many of our leading actors have studied with nearly all of the great Method teachers. Often these actors have assimilated and integrated both the inner and outer principles of Method acting, making it difficult to tell which of their teachers have had the greatest influence on them.

In our pluralistic times, why should there not be more than one acting style? Certainly, we appreciate the diversity that exists in painting, music, dance, sculpture, and architecture. As Clurman said in regard to the Method, there are many ways to practice it and none of them can profess to be the gospel truth. He is supported in this belief by Adler, who said that the Stanislavski Method can be the means for numerous acting styles. Stanislavski himself believed that art is in a constant state of change, and that the artist should feel free to alter existing theories and techniques. He urged his American disciples to find their own way, and this is precisely what they did. The permanent influence of the Method in America has resulted from the interweaving of their individual and creative personalities with the basic Stanislavski principles. Method principles are reflected in the acting and teaching of many—even those who would deny any association with it.

In art, knowledge and traditions are constantly changing, offering boundaries to be broken. Any creative form derives its vital essence from the sudden shifts that keep occurring because of artistic individualities. In some way, I hope this book will enrich your own individuality.

PART I
THE TECHNIQUE
OF METHOD
ACTING

Part I

The Technique of Method Acting

THE FORCE OF INNER INTENTIONS

No interpretation takes place without the use of actions or intentions, and all actors use them consciously or unconsciously. Actions refer not only to the physical behavior of a character; the rich meaning of actions also encompasses the inner thoughts, emotions and feelings of the character. The conscious use of actions enables the actor to have pinpoint clarity about the character's intentions. Since certain feelings pass through the writer in arriving at specific actions, you must repeat that process in order to capture the writer's meaning. This is accomplished by a line by line analysis of the script for either a stage or film production.

A general acquaintance with a script is gained as the actor reads it and permits it to arouse feelings and ideas spontaneously. After that, the actor has the responsibility for discovering a character's actions. Identifying a character's actions enables the actor to plan the human behavior of the character, based on a precise knowledge of what the character is wishing, wanting and willing at any given moment. With this knowledge, the actor has organic justifications for the logic of a character's activities.

An action justifies an actor's presence in a situation—and establishes the right to be in the situation. Stella Adler constantly asserts that one does not go on stage to act, but to do actions. An action alone, she emphasizes, does not enable you to act; it is the knowledge you have about the action which will lead you to richer acting results. There are no lines, just actions, and the lines come out of the action. The more doable the action, the more the words of the script will be experienced through the action. An important element in the Adler approach to the action is to make it personal by asking: Where have I done it? Where have I seen it? If you have not experienced the action by having done it or seen it, you then try to imagine the action. By imagining an action, you can often develop aspects of your talent that perhaps never completely existed before. Finally, Adler points out that it is necessary to gain ownership of your character's actions by creating the experience of action.

How do you formulate your actions? Verbs should be used to formulate actions because they are more doable. Nouns should be avoided, since they deal with states of feeling and can lead to imitation and conventional results. It is extremely helpful to state your actions in an interesting way which captures the psychology of the character. What kind of language would the character use to describe the action in a circumstance? In analyzing a script, you may first arrive at actions that have a literal interpretation, but an immeasurable vigor can be added by reconstructing the action with a character's colloquialisms. For example, the action "to search" is not as imaginative and doable as "to tear this room apart." You can make actions that seem difficult more immediate by placing an "I wish" before them.

Harold Clurman once was asked how he had such tremendous knowledge of a play and his answer was, "Because I read the play!" After studying a role line by line, the actor can be sure the right actions have been selected. The words of a script are communicating specific things, and you must be openly receptive to the impulses that the words should arouse. The actions exist in the circumstances and when you place yourself in the circumstances, you should permit your imagination to take flight in order to arrive at the most interesting actions. Adler further suggests that you should stay away from the words of a script until you feel ownership of the actions.

Actions dictate the number of sections in the role. You analyze and break down a script into sections by first determining the actions. Some actions will span a short period of time, and others can be quite lengthy. Actions are not to be dealt with in an arbitrary way; instead, each action change must be fully justified. An action for any given section remains the same as long as the lines are applicable to the action. When the lines are no longer applicable, a new section begins and a new action arises. A section ends because the action has been fulfilled or not fulfilled. In either case, a new action is needed. With film scripts, each shot does not dictate a change of action. If the lines are applicable, an action can cover a series of shots.

In film work, the action is a lifeline; it affords the actor the control and concentration needed to deal with the technical disruptions of film making. By determining a character's actions, you can perform the role completely out of sequence—as is often required by production schedules. As long as you are aware of the action of each shot, you can avoid vagueness about the role, even if the shot is broken up over several days.

An actor's analysis of a role may involve the identification of a main action, or what is sometimes called the super-objective. This main action can be broken up into smaller actions. The smaller actions constitute the score of a role, and give specificity to each moment. In his workshop classes, Clurman gave the following example of a main action broken up into smaller actions:

"For a long portion of a script, a character may be solely concerned with one main action: he wants to avoid paying a debt. He may begin by amplifying his present inability to pay the debt; this can be a smaller action to the main action. However, he may fail to put off the other character to whom he owes the debt and then may try to find reasons in their personal relationship as to why he should not be pressed to pay the debt. This approach may also fail so that the character is compelled to imply that he is not only unable to pay the debt, but hints that the only alternative, under the circumstances, is to sever the relationship. Throughout, the main action has remained the same. Breaking it into smaller actions simply gives the main action more variety. The main action pulls together all the smaller actions into a cohesive whole. It is the sauce that is poured over a variety of ingredients. There are certain subtleties in the use of an action that are of great value. The use of an action is creatively strengthened when you perceive how the action is impeded by the situation and other characters. An action avoids being colorless when you uncover difficulties in accomplishing the action. Making adjustments fortifies the nature of the circumstances in which you are attempting to accomplish the action."

What of the moment between actions? Obviously, if an action is accomplished, a residual effect has to be shown, brief as it may be. It is what is called finishing an action. Too often, an actor is inclined to not take the brief moment to show with what satisfaction the action has been achieved, or the dissatisfaction with which it has failed. This fulfillment or frustration is an integral part of the action itself. It gives the action a finish before the next action takes over, and actually determines the manner in which the next action begins. This is basic human behavior and to ignore it is to omit those little touches that add immeasurably to the reality of your work.

THE SENSORY NETWORK

As an actor with Method techniques among your other skills, you seek to stimulate a feeling required by the script by reliving or recreating a similar emotion. Some Method actors accomplish this by using either imaginative actions or sensorial choices that have a personal, experiential meaning. Other Method actors use actions in combination with strong and specific sensory choices. It simply becomes a matter of experimenting with various Method approaches until you discover which principles work best for your acting instrument. As with any growth program in which you are being adventurous, you keep what you need and discard what you don't need.

The senses are your tools as much as your voice, speech and physical self. The senses can be harnessed and strengthened to create truthful realities. Sense memory stirs the unconscious where nine-tenths of creativity lies. The sense organs have been referred to as the organs of concentration since it is through the sensory use of the self that you concentrate. Sense memory teaches you how to create the physical, as well as the inner life of a character. Since your main concern is searching for behavior, sense memory training serves a definite purpose. Through the retraining of the senses, your individuality is sharpened. Creative use of the senses can also induce behavior and colors that are not part of your personality. Sense memory exercises can also be a powerful catalyst in dissolving mannerisms in order that fresh expressiveness can occur.

Work with sense memory employs creative exercises which call upon the senses of sight, sound, taste, touch and smell. Highly gifted actors have described how creative sensory exercises enabled them to refine their acting instruments, and attest to their value in keeping the instrument in tune. Pianists, dancers and singers devote many hours of the day to their creative gifts, even when the gift is working well. The amount of time you spend depends on the extent you wish to perfect a gift and keep it in shape.

At the Actors Studio, and in his private workshop, Lee Strasberg unceasingly spoke of history's great actors and their moments of magical inspiration. Sense memory exercises attempt to reach for the magic of inspirational acting. Some feel it is the true way of letting things happen with interesting naturalism.

LETTING GO AND BEING CENTERED

Before beginning the exercises which initiate the flow of creativity, many performers need to prepare through some form of unwinding or relaxation technique. It is a way of tuning up your instrument. It is not surprising that many well-known actors devote the necessary time to relaxation. They realize that the presence of any physical or mental battles can create obstacles to the natural flow of feelings. Numerous people for whom psychiatric therapy was not the answer will attest to the benefits of a relaxation or meditation technique.

Many cultures of the world have long been concerned with ways of relaxation, and every present day growth program includes it. The paths are many but the desired goals are similar. For any actor wishing to acquire the benefits of a relaxed body and mind, there is no shortage of specialized teachers and books. Useful books which will help start and/or advance your quest are:

Total Meditation: Mind Control Techniques for a Small Planet in Space, by Raymond van Over
The Inner Game of Tennis, by Timothy Gallwey
The Method of Zen, by Eugen Herrigel
Zen in the Art of Archery, by Eugen Herrigel
The Silent Pulse, by George Leonard
Gesture of Balance, by Tarthang Tulku
The Observing Self, by Arthur J. Deikman
Halfway Through the Door, by Alan Arkin
Zen Mind, Beginner's Mind, by Shunryu Suzuki
The Relaxation Response, by Herbert Benson

Talent has a difficult time getting through physical and mental tension. Often, the true nature of an actor's talent is seen for the first time once the actor is able to relax and let go. Actors who posture, behave like cardboard cutouts, or are called "stiff," in all likelihood are unable to relax. On the other hand, there are well-trained and experienced actors who never reinforced their talents with principles of relaxation, but suddenly discover the need and benefits.

Relaxation for the actor opens up the instrument, enabling it to become more expressive and allowing sensitivity to rise easily. Phoney results can take place when your nerves are not relaxed and under your command. With a relaxed acting instrument, convincing realities emerge more easily. An actor who is victimized by inhibited sensitivity can realize more sensitive expressiveness by mastering relaxation; otherwise, the sensitivity remains locked up where it is of little use. The ultimate aim of relaxation is a point of physical and mental awareness that enables one to recognize tension when it occurs and immediately deal with it. Relaxation, then, must be achieved as part of your preparation for the creative state, but also has to be maintained while you are performing. Tensions can creep in during performance, and the actor should have useful means of sending unforceful mental commands to areas where this tension resides. An actor does not stop a performance while taking care of tensions. Just as a skillful violinist can tune the violin in the middle of the performance of a difficult concerto, an actor with well-developed relaxation skills can eliminate tension without interrupting a performance. There are always moments during pauses and nonverbal intervals when an actor can accomplish this. We can compare this process to painters or sculptors who clean their brushes and tools while people are watching them work. The actor entering into a creative state needs the ability, often on a moment's notice, to wipe out all mental and physical tensions in order to start with a clean canvas, painting on the canvas the precise emotional colors desired.

A distinction has to be made between energy and unnecessary energy. This, perhaps, is the most central issue in relaxation. The actor cannot relax to the extent of becoming flaccid, nor have so much energy that the muscles become taut and tightened. A certain balance has to be achieved so that the proper amount of energy can be released into whatever is required at a given perfor- mance moment in terms of emotion, movement, handling of objects and other performance details.

An actor needs to know how to control and handle the

tension that enters into a performance during high moments. It is conceivable that you may be humanly unable to prevent the emergence of tension; however, it is crucial that you recognize what is happening and have the ability to remove tension. Big emotional scenes require a lot of energy. When the instrument has the proper amount of relaxation, it will function in a way which permits the easy flow of thoughts, feelings and emotions.

Relaxation is directly related to the muscles which, unfortunately, participate in mannerisms that are creative liabilities. Through relaxation the actor can attend to and learn to control the muscles which produce undesirable mannerisms. The creative reward from this control comes when mannerisms can be converted into fresh and spontaneous expressions. There are about 600 muscles making up half of the body's weight, and all are capable of producing mannerisms. These muscles have two sets of nerves, one coming from the brain and the other carrying messages to the brain. Relaxation enables you to give the commands necessary to attain whatever degree of energy you require to create desired results. The two sets of nerves (described as a two-way street) endow the actor with the ability to accomplish this end.

Self-hypnosis, aerobics, biofeedback, visualization, massage, progressive muscle relaxation, techniques of muscular contraction and release, jogging, and any exercise or sport are some of the many forms of relaxation. The chief objective of an actor's relaxation should not be a deep transcendental pleasantness, but rather a state of creative preparation.

CHOICES

A choice is the technique means that you select in order to evoke emotion and behavior. Adler puts it quite well when she says that since the talent of an actor is very dependent on choices, the actor would be wise to have many choices. Marlon Brando, her foremost student, is known to work with as many as thirty choices in his preparation for a role, but then will only select a few that can work repeatedly. His greatness is his willingness to select challenging choices and then surrender himself to them.

Your use of this technique will be more effective if your gut-level intuition leads you to good choices. Shakespeare, for example, surely had many possibilities for shaping any particular line of dialogue, but always chose what he felt to be the best. An actor, or any artist, with a great sense of freedom will invariably have an enormous amount of choices. In researching a role, you can amass an arsenal to choose from and naturally will select those which are particularly affecting.

For many Method actors, choices are ingrained in their technique through the sensory exercises. These choices feed the imagination and enable you to avoid acting cliches. What gives the use of a choice its appealing spontaneity are the unplanned results. You do not strive for planned results but become involved with the choice at the moment it is being created. This gives the moment the human quality of behavior happening for the first time.

You can have a multitude of ideas that keep burbling up in the mind; choices provide the means of making them specific. At times, you will employ many choices in order to instill a moment with different dimensions of a character's personality. The simultaneous use of several choices reflects the complexities, opposites and contradictory elements in human behavior. At other times, you will discover that a more focused concentration, using fewer choices, will be more desirable.

THE LIFE IN OBJECTS

The actor is constantly connecting with different kinds of objects. In a stage performance, when you may have to be on stage for a long period of time, your attention goes from one object to another. This gives a structural unity to your performance. In a film performance, you still deal with objects, perhaps a few in quick shots and more in longer shots. For both film and stage, however, you should imbue objects with a life of their own and permit them to become part of a character's behavior.

Objects are found in the writer's situations and characters. You can add immeasurably to the objects by complicating them. You complicate an object by, for example, having to deal with the sleeves of a coat that are inside out before you can put it on. As an exercise, select daily objects and try to complicate them: a door, a letter, shoes, kitchen utensils, magazines, etc. In this way, you not only learn some of the basic principles of pulling things out of a script, but also give greater life to your performance.

A table or another piece of furniture between two people having a confrontation can become very active. It can be a barrier of some kind or it can become symbolically personal. Using your imagination, you can transform the table or chair into a different object which gives the moment more liveliness in terms of character and situation. Your environment can become a fantasy object. A party can become an insane asylum and all the people in it become crazy inmates.

Whether you are using objects for their actual properties or turning them into imaginary objects, the process of exploration is identical. That process involves a creation of sensory realities: what the object looks like; how it affects the sense of touch, smell and taste; in what way it arouses certain memories and experiences.

An object in a scene can become something else by transforming it into an object that has personal meaning. Objects can sometimes have abstract meanings—such as a dish or pencil—but through imagination you can permit the object to be something other than what it is. This is what is referred to in Method acting as a substitutional object. No one need know the personal meanings attached to this process; an audience is only concerned with its dramatic results. A sheet of paper, therefore, can become whatever your fantasy and imagination wishes it to become—it can become the skin of a person or the material of a garment with significant memories. What matters is that the substitution helps the scene. Objects can even become the personal property of a person that you know or do not know. An object can be the possession of a relative or friend; or even a general, president, movie star or Pope.

You first look for the objects relevant to the beginning of a scene and then pass from one object to another. If you are stymied for a first object, then anything can become an object. A chair on the set can be observed to come up with answers about its height, weight, texture of wood and material, period or style. This will provide the necessary springboard to reach for more meaningful objects.

The way in which you regard atmospheric objects can aid enormously in attaining a certain character value. An entire set can become an atmosphere of hate, love, fear or loneliness. In order to accomplish this, you regard the objects as being objects of hate, love, fear and loneliness. This can happen just as it does in your daily life when you have days during which everything around you is colored by your feelings: a sunny day will be gloomy if you feel gloomy; a gloomy day can be joyful if you are feeling joyful.

THE MAGICAL *AS IF*

The *As If* is used effectively by both actors and directors as well as medical students, tennis players, scientific researchers and everyone. Graduate medical students, for example, pursuing studies in clinical work, will imagine themselves to have symptoms of a malady.

The *As If* works particularly well when the organic impulses of an actor have been well trained. In an untrained talent, the quality of physical aliveness that is created with this tool can sometimes result, unfortunately, in posturing attitudes. Nevertheless, it is useful at any time providing that there is an awareness of its conventional traps.

The *As If* can help actors and directors to give a particular tone to a scene. There may be a scene, for example, requiring an element of eeriness, that takes place in a living room at five o'clock in the afternoon. In order to get the eerie element, the director can appeal to the imagination of the actors and ask them to think of the scene *As If* it were taking place in a graveyard or deserted warehouse at four o'clock in the morning.

An *As If* can lead to a physical characterization. Shirley MacLaine was able to completely realize a character when she thought of the character's walk *As If* she were walking on eggs.

A character can have an overwhelming anxiety about entering a room. The actor can approach the moment *As If* there might be a booby trap and the door might explode when opened. Every moment, in some way, is full of *As If* choices.

Children use imagination to a remarkable extent in games so that they can experience something *As If* it were really occurring. It is not beyond the actor's ability to do the same. You simply program yourself and permit it to happen.

Dwell upon the sensations and behavior that the following *As If* examples can arouse:

As If I had just returned from cross-country skiing.

As If I just woke up after only a little sleep
and someone is screaming at me.

As If I am in a beautiful place and a fawn is being born and I am also hearing a bulldozer.

As If I had just won an Emmy, Oscar or Tony Award.

As If I have been in a hot bus station for 12 hours.

As If I were in a forest clearing at midday.

VISUALIZING ANOTHER PERSON AND IMAGES

Personalization is a Method acting technique tool which can be easily used by actors with no Method acting training or only a slight interest in it. Personalization is done by selecting facial or physical features of a person you know who arouses the same emotion in you as that of a character playing opposite you. It can be the color of an actor's eyes which reminds you of someone who arouses love, anger, fear, hate or any of the primary emotions. It can be the actor's hair, nose, way of walking or even total physical appearance.

The preceding defines the most common application for personalization although it does have other uses. The use of images, for example, is widely accepted for personalization. Some believe that the actor should have personal images for everything done with a role, and that the actor employing images should try to find events of a personal nature from life that will correspond to various events in the role. Often, the events borrowed from life may have absolutely no bearing on what is actually happening in a scene but you can, through imaginative concentration, get a vital and truthful experience.

The images that are most frequently used are remembered experiences of personal events which the actor imposes upon situations dictated by the script. For example, you encounter a scene in which a loved one is sick and dying. You can think of a time when you saw a loved one mortally ill. Another example would be a situation in which there is a certain kind of relationship to another character. The other character could be a movie tycoon, a wealthy heiress, a great athlete, a figure of royalty or whatever. You may have never encountered anyone like this, but you may know people who have the approximate traits of these types. You can personalize them for any of the types mentioned.

Personalization can be quite useful in a professional circumstance in which negative feelings exist between actors, making it difficult for one or both actors to accept each other in a positive scene. Since this can affect the flow of a performance, an actor may use a positive personalization for the other actor.

Another type of personalization uses the way you actually feel about having a grubby apartment, soiled shoes, unfashionable clothes, etc. If a character has unfashionable clothes and is experiencing a despondency that has nothing to do with unfashionable clothes, you could personalize the unfashionable clothes as being your own and use the despondency it causes you in life to wear such clothes. In this way, you personalize something that has meaning for you in life to capture the feeling that your character is experiencing. As an exercise, make a list of the life circumstances that arouse certain attitudes and feelings in you that can be used at some time or the other.

SENDING IN A SUBSTITUTE

Another Method acting tool which is quickly understood is substitution. There are two types of substitution: using a substitutional situation involves taking an event from your life and substituting it for a parallel event in the script; using a substitutional object generally means transforming a prop into an object that has personal meaning for you. However, there are times when the use of a substitutional object need not have a personal meaning. Jerzy Grotowski dramatically used substitutional objects in his work at the Polish Laboratory Theatre. His actors transformed floors into sand or an ocean; an object of metal took on human qualities; a prison cell was imagined through the sticks of a chair.

Substitutions, personalizations and images are closely related and the terminology is loosely used. Nevertheless, understanding these principles should offer you valuable information about how to use them effectively in your own way.

DIALOGUE FROM YOUR INTERIOR

Inner dialogue, or inner monologue, is a means of using your own inner feelings to give behavioral feelings for moments in a role. Inner dialogues of all kinds are constantly going on within the most private part of yourself; they have particular kinds of energy which can be used in a performance. Without question, the use of inner dialogue can help you sustain a character's inner feelings.

Actors will paraphrase their dialogue in order to arrive at the various meanings underneath the spoken words. This is called working with the subtext, a form of investigating inner dialogue, which helps the actor to create a logical line for the role. The most powerful use of inner dialogue is when you dwell upon private thoughts that are related to the emotional content of a scene. During this process, you speak the author's lines and at the same time you engage in an accompanying silent dialogue specifically dealing with a real life situation. The concentration required here may seem unusual, but one uses as much concentration to engage in different levels of day-to-day dialogue. Deep inner thought of a remarkable nature is often achieved with the use of a personal inner dialogue, even though it may be at variance with the spoken dialogue.

Inner dialogue continually occurs when we deal with our concerns and problems. You can also detect it in other people, e.g., seeing someone make an extraordinary effort to keep strong feelings inside in order to prevent an argument.

A technical concern is the length, rhythm and tone of the inner dialogue you have personally chosen for a character. The rhythm and tone of your inner dialogue should match the character's dialogue and if the length of your inner dialogue is shorter than the character's dialogue, you can simply repeat words and phrases.

BE AN ANIMAL

Although the animal exercise is concerned with imitating what one has observed about animals, it is not animal antics or mimicking that are important clues for creating a character. Hopping about, scratching, searching or slithering movements should not be regarded as most important. The exercise can easily result in ridiculous cliches if your concern is only with the physical movements and gestures. The thousands of non-human species are fascinating to us because each one is so different and unpredictable. You should also study the inner life of an animal when doing the exercise. When the inner life is created by selective traits, you will discover that it can be a useful tool in your arsenal of choices.

When we speak of people as being fearless as a lion, scared as a mouse, having the light movement of a spider, nervous as a cat, lumbering as a bear, majestic as an ostrich, moving with the insinuating composure of a tiger, light as a gazelle, sly as a fox, lazy as a whale, possessed with the energetic playfulness of a dolphin or as fleeting as a hummingbird, we are using common similes. But the exercise would be of little use if you were only concerned about the totally physical behavior that these characteristics convey. That kind of concern is conventionally used by misinterpreters of the exercise.

You should ultimately be concerned with using one or two traits of an animal. You can discover a different physical self as the exercise gives character meaning to areas and parts of the body. Sometimes the exercise can do wonders for areas of uninteresting expressiveness.

SAVORING EACH MOMENT

Jack Lemmon reveals how at one time he would vigorously attack a role and "beat it to death with a stick," but now relaxes and permits each moment to take care of itself. This has to do with the moment-to-moment concern in acting. An entire role is a string of individual moments. In its truest sense, moment-to-moment investigation conveys the process of perfecting a role. It can often be a powerful means to uncover deep hidden meanings that otherwise might elude the actor. Directors will sometimes devote entire rehearsals to encourage actors to fully explore each line of dialogue through endless means: paraphrasing, inner monologue, relationships, choices, etc. This moment-to-moment process can lead to useful discoveries and give a scene the dimension it needs.

Moment-to-moment investigation requires an open awareness of the unique existence of each moment. With this kind of approach you have the feeling of being able to have absolute freedom in a moment without being concerned about the nuances of the next moment. It is being aware of what precisely is occurring in the moment. It is often referred to as "living in the now."

PRIVATE MOMENT AS A SOLO PSYCHODRAMA

The power of an actor's public solitude lies in the ability to be unaware of the audience and totally concentrate on the event of the dramatic situation. By doing so, the actor draws the audience into what is transpiring. Every actor attempts to involve the spectator. What matters is to what degree the actor reveals the inner personal depths that give remarkable power to certain moments. You may have already discovered that releasing your own private thoughts can be a way of giving true meaning to your acting. Some performers have said that they find it more fulfilling to announce their private thoughts in public than behind the closed doors of a psychoanalyst's office.

The less you are aware of an audience, the more power you have over the audience as you involve it in the private event which you are publicly creating. The audience, in other words, has become essentially nonexistent for you and, therefore, imposes no demands. The private moment exercise enables you to create deep private feelings with the flow that is only possible when you are completely alone. This is a professional condition that should be present in your work for it enables you to avoid the conventional trap of demonstrating to an audience or camera. Conventional actors employ numerous subtle means to acknowledge the fact that they are being observed, often to the extreme of some form of seductive titillation.

I. Rapaport, an early Stanislavski disciple, created a version of the private moment exercise which he called an exercise of public solitude. In his exercise, the actor was surrounded by objects from his private room and had to carry out the kind of activities that one often does when alone: writing a letter, rehearsing a role, sewing a button, etc. Rapaport's exercise is more a personal moment than a private moment, since one might not necessarily stop such activities if someone entered the room, although the dynamics might be altered because of that person's sudden presence. In attempting to find a way of creating an exercise that would deal more specifically with problems of public solitude, Strasberg wondered what an actor could do in a workshop that in life was so private that the activity would stop the moment someone entered a room. From the beginning, he noticed that actors achieved concrete results with his version of the private solitude exercise. Actors, who previously had problems with blocked emotions, inhibition, concentration and even vocal difficulties, derived immediate benefits.

Many actors find it difficult to do the private moment exercise because they believe they do not have any private moments of dramatic interest, but there are many personal moments that can be used as a substitute. As a way of preparation for the private moment exercise, the personal moment can be useful.

You may find the private moment a challenge since it contends with very strong moments of privacy in which you deal with rage, shattering sadness, vulgarities, etc. In the permissive setting of a serious workshop, the challenge of the exercise can be diminished as one observes the extraordinary revelations and insightful impact that others derive from it.

Acting coaches who have used the exercise have observed extremely individual realities: uncovering problems of crying and laughter; finding clues for releasing erotic impulses; experiencing anger for the first time; discovering how one can downgrade oneself in moments of privacy; being able to create a strong natural inner life simply by being alone and doing absolutely nothing. There can be the discovery, for whatever reason, that contact with personal possessions and sentimental objects can have more sensitivity than contact with people. All these discoveries can be useful in solving both artistic and personal problems. In my acting workshop, I never have an actor do the private moment exercise until I feel that the actor has developed sufficiently in the work and is ripe for the enlightenment the exercise can offer. I cannot overpraise its capacity for giving an actor new insights—both psychological and artistic illuminations.

It is no easy matter for a person to reveal a moment of complete privacy. These can be moments of inner struggle which sometimes cannot be controlled, but somehow the exercise helps one to cope with the emotional impact of such moments. There are impulses of many kinds that can only be fulfilled in complete privacy and some can even be too private to be used in the exercise.

The private moment is sometimes referred to as being equivalent to the star pause when the actor is alone, with or without words, and something decisive is happening. The film medium is particularly rich in these moments, specifically during those times when the camera is focused on an actor enacting an event in complete solitude.

As a scene choice, there sometimes has been gross misuse

of this exercise by actors who totally ignore their responsibility to convey vocally and emotionally. One must not get this involved with digging into one's private life without having the technique to clearly convey the experience within the situation of the written scene. It is important that you do not hold onto the experience of the exercise when you use its emotional energy for a scene. The exercise is misused if you do not find the means to permit it to go into a situation. By analyzing the exercise, moment-to-moment, you can discover many details that can be effectively employed for specific moments in a scene. Choices can be uncovered from the ingredients of the exercise which can be used, for example, in selecting sensorial feelings or handling objects in a scene.

Sometimes, one's individual style can be uncovered through the exercise. During the exercise, I witnessed an extremely talented actor develop the basis for an individual style that encompassed elements of charm and comedy, characteristics of an articulate redneck, as well as traits for a macho-clown type. When his behavior during the exercise had been analyzed, he took the exercise a step further by permitting the behavior to become character elements in an improvisational scene.

Because of the exercise, an actress in my workshop was finally able to come to terms with the fact that, for her entire adult life, she had been denying the sensual beauty of her body. During the exercise, she was alone in her room and experimented with makeup, selected clothes which revealed her lovely contours, exercised her strong body, etc. Thereafter, she began to relate to men in a completely different manner. The value of the exercise occurred because of her willingness to explore her most private feelings. New expressive powers were unleashed in her acting (as well as in her personal life) because she fulfilled the challenge of the exercise.

Becoming acquainted with the nature of the exercise

can also lead you to living out the private moments of a character you are developing. In that way, you can uncover unexpected details that you might have overlooked otherwise.

For numerous actors, releasing emotions in a private way is the very essence of their acting. The private moment exercise can help one set the guidelines to permit emotional energy to easily flow. The first time you do the exercise may result in just taking a stab at it, but you can also discover that you are on the right track for further work with it.

AFFECTIVE MEMORY: DIGGING INTO YOUR PRIVATE VAULT

Affective memory (sometimes referred to as emotional memory or emotional recall) is a tool used by some Method actors to recapture a feeling that occurred during a highly emotional experience. The actor attempts to recreate an experience by recalling the sensations associated with the strong event. At a primary level, this is accomplished by stimulating sensory realties in order to relive the event. Affective memories are interwoven with the emotional fabric of life experiences. They are always with us, constantly surfacing into our consciousness and determining our actions, thoughts and feelings.

Strasberg always cautioned that the exercise should not be done by a person with a severe emotional disturbance as it may only result in feeding the disturbance.

You may find this exercise useful; you may want to discard it in preference to other technique tools available to you. Not every affective memory that is attempted will work and be useful. It is a matter of experimentation and much can be accomplished in the quest to find out what emotional experiences can be called upon to create an emotional impact. Strasberg said that an actor may try 100 affective memories and discover that only 6 really work. Although Adler strongly disapproves of this exercise, Clurman believed that it is an indispensable exercise as an element in training. He said that it is an exercise during which you get under an emotion without being sure as to what it will produce: laughter may result when tears are expected, and vice versa.

As with the private moment, the affective memory has to be artistically fused with character and situation, otherwise it can wander off into a totally unrelated area. How is the affective memory used properly in performance? This has much to do with an actor's sensitivity. A truly sensitive and creative actor need not indulge in a long involved process to recapture a deeply buried strong emotion. One merely selects events from one's life history to discover how to unlock them with the golden keys offered by the exercise. The process of selection may involve careful investigation either in privacy and/or under the guidance of a perceptive teacher. After a particular affective memory is used once or twice, you need only to recall one or two major details (it can be something sensorial) to quickly produce the desired emotion.

PART II
TECHNIQUE
EXERCISES

Part II

Technique Exercises

INTRODUCTION TO THE EXERCISES

An actor's main career concern is the search for behavior. Sense memory training has long served a definite creative purpose in helping actors to extend their behavioral technique. The exercises establish the principles of searching for new forms of experience and transplanting them back into acting. So, these are exercises that enable you to creatively experiment and expand. By assuming the responsibility to use your acting instrument more expressively, you are not acquiring a steamer trunk full of tricks; instead, you develop a meaningful technique with appealing human qualities. Acting is a natural function and an actor in thoughtful technique training learns how to do away with interferences so that the true nature of talent can surface. The experience of the exercises can be a fabulous one as you discover new uses of your senses, as well as new facts about them. The exercises, then, are tools of self-study, an opportunity to observe yourself in a completely different way.

Sensorial technique exercises have an uncommon way of creating your own individuality, a characteristic in all actors of high professional status —"stars," if you wish to call them that.

For each exercise, you should select an action from the list in the appendix or an action of your own choice. You can elaborate on the action by giving it a story, a dramatic situation. You may even have a situation in mind—a scene from a play or movie, a situation from a newspaper story, etc. This will help you to put the exercises to immediate and practical use.

Make a list of strong experiences you have had with the senses. This will help you select material for the exercises. Also make a list of a variety of actions so that you explore different emotions and feelings.

Precede the exercise by preparing yourself with the relaxation exercise in the appendix. It can be a short time of letting go and unwinding; it can be a deeper period of relaxation, if you wish.

Approach the sensory exercises with the thought in mind that you are not interested in imitating an experience, but recreating it. You will discover that locked-up emotions and impulses will surface and you should permit them to be released. It may astonish you, when you let yourself go with a strong emotion, that you can even have control over it. Like a downhill skier who flows with the perils of a run, you maintain amazing control. Be aware of the enormity of some of your emotional experiences in exercise choices, and work with them in such a way that you lead them and do not allow them to take you where they want to go. Selectivity and concentration, therefore, are important ingredients. The concentration must be controlled and one must determine how much concentration is needed. It has been noted that some people use such intense concentration with their choices that instead of creating some form of reality, they end up creating something unreal.

Letting yourself go with a strong emotion means exactly what it says—to let go, but there are numerous degrees of the letting go experience. Sometimes it is a matter of cutting down in order to arrive at desirable results. When Michelangelo was asked how he created his David, he said, "I just cut down until I found him." When you tone down a strong experience to experiment with how it can be used on a lower, confined film level, it is important not to lose the essence of the experience when it was occurring at its strongest moment.

As you begin to work with the senses, you may find that in acting, as in other aspects of life, some senses function more strongly than others. The exercises will teach you how much truth and energy is needed. In certain moments, a lesser percentage of organic truth might be preferable to pouring out your emotions. The exercise work will nurture the degree of logic at your command to establish a sense of truthful naturalness.

HOT LIQUID/COLD LIQUID

The exercises with a hot or cold liquid contain all the rudiments of Method technique exercises which explore the senses. Select an action that has to do with naturalness and simple truths since these initial exercises are intended for an exploration of your basic qualities. Preferably select beverages that you drink in the morning such as tea, cocoa, coffee, cold juices or even mineral water.

As you complete your relaxation, float easily into the exercise. (With all the exercises, there should not be a line of demarcation between when the relaxation ends and the sensory work begins.) An imaginary glass or cup should be on an imaginary table in front of you; the table should be close enough so that you never need to reach out for the object when you later pick it up. Do not rush, but give sufficient time for thorough exploration. You can drink a liquid in a few minutes, but the sensorial exploration can last as long as you wish.

Without seeing the glass or cup, or while your eyes are still gently closed at the end of the relaxation, let a sense of smell begin to awaken your other senses. Gradually, permit the object to slowly come into focus and begin to distinguish its essential features—the shape, colors and design. Note any distinguishing feature, such as a little crack or chip. Truly make an effort to see the object before you make actual tactile contact.

Be precise concerning the object's location by placing your palm over a steaming cup (while working with a hot liquid) and sensing the heat on your palm. Place your fingertips very close to the object and without touching it, feel the warmth. With a cold liquid, put your fingers gently into the liquid and feel its coolness on your fingertips. Be concerned with one simple reality at a time and try not to explore all the senses immediately. The exercise is accumulative in nature—you explore one sensory reality and retain it as you go on to another. If you feel that you are losing a reality, try to get it back and keep exploring other realities so that you have, by the end of the exercise, an amalgam of experienced senses.

Pick up the object, but be aware of any tension in your shoulder muscles or your arm as you pick it up. As you begin to move it from one hand to another, establish a rhythm which is neither too fast nor too slow. As you move the object, explore it and come up with answers about its texture and weight. Find out about the sound vibrations of the object as you tap your fingers against it. Shift the cup or glass back and forth, trying to get a sense of the liquid as it goes from one side to the other. When you place the object on your arm, sense its temperature. Bring the object close to the lips, again ensuring that no tension occurs in the shoulders. Feel the cold or heat near your lips and be aware of the aroma as you prepare to explore the taste more deeply. Taste the liquid, first exploring it on your lips and the tip of your tongue; sip it again and sense the taste with the middle, sides and back of your tongue. Try not to savor the liquid with obvious mouth movements as that may tend to "act out" the experience rather than letting it occur naturally. Swallow the liquid and slowly feel it go down the esophagus into the stomach. What effect does the warmth or coolness create as it travels along the ten-inch esophagus route to the stomach?

Set down the object and explore the sensations you have created thus far and observe to what extent they are capturing the meaning of your action. Localizing the taste on the tip of the tongue will, perhaps, give a different meaning to your action than when you localize it in the stomach.

Pick up the object again and place it near your face, without touching the face, and feel the warmth or coolness emanating from it; then touch parts of your face and head with the object. Move the object to the neck, chest or stomach. Feel the sensation through the material of your clothing and establish the difference between that sensation and the sensation you felt on the skin of your neck and face. With your imagination, place the object on your thighs or between your legs, and you will recall that you sometimes place the object in unusual places to get warmth or coolness.

At times, look away from the object and have faith that it is there. Move the object towards your head and explore the sense of smell in more detail. Permit the sense of smell to fill the head area and then move into other parts of the body—the shoulders, arms and torso.

Finally, put the object on the table and let it disappear. Take a few minutes to simply sit and become aware of what senses are still aroused from the exercise and how they are fulfilling the meaning of your action.

Become aware of an everyday experience having more sensations than you realized. Try not to imitate the everyday activity by "acting" or pretending, but get your own reality in a simple truthful way. Regard the initial exercises not as mundane, but as the beginning of your creative development in the sensorial use of yourself.

MAKEUP/SHAVING/GROOMING

This exercise entails getting a sense of yourself by visualizing yourself in an imaginary mirror while using imaginary objects to put on makeup, shave or groom yourself.

Following the relaxation, and with an action in mind, begin to get a sense of yourself in an imaginary mirror. With your hands, create the frame of the mirror and the surface of the glass. (Later, if you open a cabinet door, create the sense of opening it and the sensory realities involved in establishing the physical properties of the shelves and the imaginary objects which rest upon them.) At this point, however, dwell mostly on your image. At times, turn your head sideways in order to vary the type of concentration needed to create a reflective image. Be aware of an awakening awareness of yourself as a physical object. As you take the necessary time to explore your image, make tactile contact with your hair and face, but do not actually touch your hair and face—just have a sense of the texture of your hair as you run your fingers through imaginary strands.

As you use the objects, attempt to go beyond their

conventional uses in order to become more involved with their endless qualities. You can, for example taste the mascara, shaving lotion, colognes and perfumes; become aware of hidden aromas of a comb or razor. As with the hot and cold liquid exercises, you are creating the ultimate sensory exploration of a daily activity.

Bring the objects towards you, with no bending of the body or head towards them. If you feel that you must move slightly towards the mirror, as you do in life, then examine the movement. Through this kind of investigation you might discover unnecessary tensions that can be present in an everyday activity.

The exercise can be done standing in front of a sink and mirror, or sitting at a makeup table. An attempt should be made to keep a sense of the precise position of the various objects as you pick them up and set them down. In this way, you maintain a logic—you do not set an object down in one place and pick it up again in another.

With your imagination, explore the objects for their hidden realities: run a finger lightly over the edge of a razor blade or the teeth of a comb, for example, and explore tactile properties with a sense of curiosity.

For women who do no use makeup, or for men who have beards, activities can be created with cleansing creams, lotions, tweezers or trimming scissors. Some women have difficulty with this exercise because they do not like makeup and do not use it, just as the exercise may be hard for some men who might avoid looking at an unwanted facial feature. In either case, look into the mirror and observe the interior emotion associated with those feelings.

SUNSHINE

This exercise relates to the numerous nerve endings on the skin that report the varied experiences of temperature and sensations created by the environment. It is important you do not try to recreate a sunburn or anything emotional. If you avoid the sun, try to create a mild negative reaction with a corresponding action such as "to get rid of."

As you complete the relaxation, begin to visualize the sun in front of you. Do not place it overhead as that can cause you to bend your head back to expose your face to the sun. The sun is an object; you should avoid moving towards it and permit it to come to you. Omit the place in which the sunshine is present by not attempting to visualize a beach, trees, sky, etc., but create only the sunshine on the face—the brow, nose and upper lip. Avoid resorting to such conventional schtick as wiping perspiration off the face and neck. If you are really perspiring, don't try to wipe it away. If you feel a stickiness, permit it to exist without fingering or pulling on your clothes. Remember, as with any other exercise, you may want to use the sensation from sunshine in a scene in which the sensation does not exist, but where it can give rich behavior to the scene by substituting a reality. Give yourself up to the experience and permit it to do whatever it wants.

As you work with the head area, turn it to one side or the other and determine the behavioral meaning that you get in terms of your action. Gradually let the sun travel down the body as it affects the throat, neck, shoulders and upper chest area. Attempt to define the sensation in those areas. As you begin to work on large areas, determine how the sun feels through your clothes. You can also imagine yourself completely naked as you receive the sensation.

Begin to use the sun on the arms and hands to explore organic gesture. What meaning in your action can you capture as you extend one or both arms and expose them to the sun? As you progress with the technique work, the exercises will help you to arrive at imaginative gestures and steer you away from mental conceptions of gestures which tend to create conventional signals.

When the sensation reaches the abdomen and pelvis areas, slide down into the chair so that your legs are outstretched. The sunshine, at this point, might create a sensual feeling as you spread your legs apart in order to get into hidden places. Lift your arms and feel the sun in the armpits. In what way are you capturing the action as you are slumped in the chair with legs apart and armpits exposed? Women sometimes get more erotic stimulation than men because the sun penetrates them in a sexual way; men, on the other hand, sometimes feel deprived of their sexual energy while exposed to the sun.

Let the sun travel down the legs, covering all the frontal areas down to the nerve endings that end in the toes. Then, create the feeling of the sunshine coming from all directions—from behind you, beneath, from the sides, overhead—so that you are completely surrounded with rays of the sun. You can now begin to investigate the use of overall sensations to create infinite ways of sitting in a chair, and explore its pertinent relation to your action as you do so. Move about in the chair, lean forward and expose your back to the sun, sit sideways, straddle the chair and let the sun warm your buttocks. Find those areas which have not been exposed such as the small of the back, private areas, back of the legs, etc. For concentrational purposes, determine if the rays from behind are stronger than the rays from the side. Various combinations of strength and weakness can be created in different body areas as you sit sideways, lean forward, etc. Capture the meaning of the action as you create sitting movements and positions.

Stand up, retaining the sitting sensations, and explore

the sun enveloping you in a standing position, even getting a sense of the sun's rays beneath your feet. Sit down again and you may discover that the sensation is different because you have explored it more fully while standing.

SHARP PAIN

This exercise gives a knowledge of how pain can have substitute realities as you create an imaginary physical pain and transfer it to behavior needed for a character experiencing an emotionally painful situation. This furthers the skill of working with substituting realities. You create a physical pain with this exercise, but the scene that you transfer it to need not involve the character experiencing a physical pain. It can be an inner emotional disturbance the character is feeling and your inner sense of an imaginary pain will give the moment the organic reality it needs.

It is important to emphasize that you must control the pain that you are recreating from a life experience; do not permit it to drift into uncontrollable screaming and hysteria. If you feel it approaching that state, withdraw to a lower level of experience. At the end of the exercise, you must turn off the pain and not permit it to linger.

The sensation of pain can be caused by a malfunctioning in a localized body area, with the resulting pain occurring deep in the tissues, organs and bones. These are preferred choices as the exercise is intended to convey an inner experience, such as an inner disturbing thought or mood. Relate the pain to the selected action. Pain can also be caused by something in the environment which threatens the body, causing cuts, burns and stings. These sensations enter into the body through the nerve fibers, beginning with the nerve endings on the skin. In either case, whether the pain comes from within or is caused from without, the painful area becomes crucial. All of the body's functioning is directed toward the painful area, after the body receives signals that something is wrong somewhere.

During the exercise, attempt to get the pain at its strongest and then manipulate it on different levels so that you have control over rising and subsiding painful feelings. You create the sharp pain by recalling the sensation of a particular pain—trusting that the senses have their own memory. Select a localized pain such as a toothache, or a pain in the side, stomach, wrist, elbow, foot, ear, shoulder, finger, etc. A headache is not an ideal choice as it is not a defined pain but tends to give a woozy feeling rather than the throbbing kind of pain in a small defined area. Headaches, particularly migraines, are painful, and they can be an effective choice in later exercises. If you select a pain in an area related to a broken bone experience, let the concentration be on the pain only and not on related memories of the event involving a place and people.

We have a variety of experiences with pain. Joggers may endure pain and discover that there is a close association between pain and pleasure—the first mile may be painful, but then pleasure takes over. For the mountain climber who each day covers a short distance, sometimes measured in yards, pain can be used for patience.

Avoid selecting an overall pain such as fatigue or an aching body. Choose a defined pain, and discover how it affects nearby areas. If you choose a toothache, explore your individual kind of response to the pain, recognizing that no person's toothache is like that of another. Original and unique behavior is created when you explore your own personal experience. If the pain spills over too much into adjoining areas, develop a means of self-correction and return the pain to its localized area.

You might actually get a tingling sensation in areas such as the arms, fingers, lips or stomach. This is caused by locked-up sensitivity being released and going into those areas. If an emotional reaction is triggered by the exercise, do not panic but control it and use it for creative expression. When there is a strong emotional experience, it may happen very strongly for a brief period. After it happens, get a sense of how it continues, even if it does so more weakly. Vary its strength in order to discover different facets of the experience. Make certain that other areas of the body are relaxed; in this way, you will begin to establish the facility to have a strong feeling in a localized area and yet be able to check tension in other areas.

The inner experience, if it is created properly, will be conveyed. How often have you seen a person sitting quietly with no movements, and yet observed a deep experience from within being conveyed through a motionless, untensed body? How often have you experienced this yourself?

The area of the pain is not to be touched or soothed. You may wish to use the pain as a behavioral element in a scene in which your character does not have a sharp pain. In this case, the pain you are creating can convey a state of anxiety, impatience (or even patience) and a variety of other values. Furthermore, soothing the imaginary pain you are creating can even cause its strength to diminish and thereby make the exercise purposeless.

Concentrate upon whatever kind of pain you are creating, even if your efforts are not succeeding. You create results through concentration. Sometimes the results do not happen, but hold on to your concentration and do not abandon it. Even though what you expect to happen is not happening, you are still creating as long as you keep the concentration going. When you abandon concentration, you abandon one of the basic creative processes of the actor. As long as the concentration is there, something is happening. Whether it measures up to your expectations or not is not the important factor to be considered.

Avoid moving (or being physical) so that the inner experience can be seen at its purest. Let the strength of the inner experience be transmitted outwardly through a relaxed body. An expression will be seen on the face even when it is relaxed; there is no need to knot your facial muscles. Even though the location of the pain is not seen, its results are manifested in the way the pain surfaces to outer regions and in the meaning expressed in the voice.

If you tend to keep the eyes closed, you remove yourself from the outer elements with which you have to relate. Relate your action and sensorial state to the outer elements you visually contact. Permit sounds to emerge—moans or groans, weeping or yelling—that are neither controlled or out of control, but spontaneous. Making sounds can be useful in shaking an unchanging physical attitude of the experience. With sounds, you can test the verbal quality that will result from the pain and its different intensities and rhythms. Sound will lessen the need to move; movement sometimes can replace unreleased sounds. Letting out sound will permit your articulation to be clear, thereby avoiding the sort of mumbling that occurs when you hold on to a pain.

Towards the end of the exercise, release the pain from its localized area and let it travel into the body. At this point, there will be movement—this is the physical expression of the pain traveling through the body. It is necessary, however, to regard this as the subsidiary experience and not the main experience. You also discover how you can control the pain by releasing it and then returning the sensation to the localized area.

SHARP TASTE

Taste, like smell, is a sense that is constant in our daily lives—a savory delight that has set your taste buds atingle, the deep lingering flavor of garlic, the sometimes bad taste of the mouth in the morning, or the taste of an invigorating wine.

Although the taste buds are located on the tongue, palate, pharnyx and tonsils, you should also probe the areas of the esophagus and stomach. There are mounds on the tongue called the papillary mounds which transport the food you eat. When you experiment with imaginary solid foods, such as cheese or a hot pepper, feel the food being carried by the papillary mounds; attempt to be specific about how certain foods change your behavior. Chocolate, for example, contains a chemical also found in the human brain which gives us an up feeling.

Practice with an actual object such as a lemon, red pepper, sharp cheese, or piece of chocolate; then practice without it. When you practice without it, you may wish to create the imaginary object by exploring its weight, texture and color as you did with objects in the initial exercises. Use your imagination and do things with the object that you might not ordinarily do such as making patterns with your teeth on the skin of a lemon. With bitter objects try not to unconsciously build resistance towards them by grimacing or by having a sour, disgusting facial expression. Permit the face to be relaxed and trust that sensory realities will be seen. Let the taste exist without smacking the lips and overusing the mouth muscles for savoring. Excessive mouth movement can tend towards imitation.

A bitter taste may turn pleasant and then bitter again; it can vacillate between bitter, not so bitter and pleasant. Whatever the sensation, pleasant or unpleasant, try to direct the experience to specific areas such as the back of the throat, along the gum ridge or the roof of the mouth.

By doing the exercise without the imaginary object, you become more concerned with how the taste is affecting the taste receptors than with the tactile properties of an imaginary object. Be aware of how food sometimes finds its way to the smell receptors since the senses of smell and taste are closely related; some even believe they are inseparable. They are our close (or inner) senses, just as sight and sound are regarded as distant (or outer) senses. As close senses, they can arouse strong emotions.

After using your concentrational abilities to localize the taste, permit it to go into the legs, arms and torso in order to further investigate pleasure or displeasure. What kind of gesture can be expressed with the taste as it goes into the arms and hands? The sense of taste, as with the sense of smell, can arouse bodily pleasure that is sometimes close to sensual pleasure; explore it in erotic areas.

Organic movements and gesture can occur at any time during exploration. It is essential to remember that they can grant you a uniqueness and individuality which help develop the rudiments of an original style.

You may work with the taste in a standing position, but be aware of how sensation determines the way in which you rise from the chair. When you sit again you may find it stronger since it may have had the opportunity to travel into the lower part of the body where there are no taste buds, but the sensation can spill over from the stomach area into the pelvis and legs. As you continue the exercise, localize it in certain responsive areas.

At intervals, particularly since taste can demonstrate to you how it colors words, have an inner dialogue related to the action; take time between the words of the inner dialogue to discover how the sensation is going into the dialogue, even if you are nonverbal. You may wish to work with this element in a verbal way so that you can hear the speech colors resulting from the taste.

In this or later exercises with taste, you might take it to its experiential limits with your fantasy as you taste colors, people and objects around you.

SHARP SMELL

Smell is a more complex sense than taste. The smell receptors are more sensitive than the taste receptors and are connected directly with that part of the brain having to do with emotions. We experience new odors every day, and these odor stimuli are immediately dealt with by the olfactory brain. Remember this when, for five minutes at the end of each day, you practice recreating significant sensory experiences of the day as a way of further sensitizing yourself. During this period, try not to feel any compulsion to work with the senses, but merely think of what experience you have had during the day which was sensorially interesting. It can be mountain air, an ocean breeze, a siren in the traffic, the fragrance of a rose, etc. When you set aside this time at the end of each day during early training, you are not wasting the five minutes, but are working towards strengthening and controlling your capacity for sense memory.

Pick an object such as a rose, disinfectant or incense; you can also select an environmental condition—sea air, smog, pollen, etc. Select a sharp smell that affects you. What kind of emotion does it create? Try not to be general and remember that there are hundreds of specific fragrances of perfumes, spices, flowers and incense. The smell of a rose can be, in its own way, just as much of a peak experience as a sexual experience. Permit yourself to be open to such experiences in the exercise work with smell and willingly become the receptacle of the elements which you have imaginarily created. The Japanese incense ritual of Kob-Do brings numerous benefits including mind expansion. Search for the choice that can expand your mind. Be aware of how one sense, such as a sharp smell, can bring the entire instrument alive with rich meaning.

Avoid keeping your head in an attitude which suggests that the smell is originating from one specific location; ideally, let the smell surround you and affect your whole being as you go deeper into the exercise.

What not easily forgotten memory can a certain smell arouse? Whatever choice you have selected, get it into the nasal nerve fibers that connect with deep layers inside the brain. If a subconscious experience is aroused, go with it.

Examples For Sharp Smell Choices

sea air	cleaning fluids	bad breath
ether	hay	disinfectants
smog	incense	deodorizers
ammonia	musty room	smelly feet
pine needles	paint	body odor
onion	kerosene	perfume
flowers	wine	cologne
garlic	beer	aftershave lotion
oregano	sweet breath	chemicals

CREATING A PLACE

Visualizing a meaningful place, vista or location, and creating its sensorial realities is the most appealing technique tool among the basic exercises because it imaginatively encompasses the entire network of the senses.

Visualization is a strong ingredient in this exercise. You

deal with visual images that stimulate you because of the way in which they have been polaroided into your memory. You can even experience "optic phenomena" during the exercise, similar to the experience of Tibetan monks, who, while sitting in caves and cells devoid of any light, begin to see their dark surroundings transformed into visuals of dazzling lights, landscapes and people. Tantric Buddhists practice seeing living pictures in the mind with results that are often more powerful than dreams. The technique principles for doing this are adopted in certain growth programs in which visualization is used to create sanctuaries to which one can retreat or escape from tensions and anxieties, or just for one's well-being. In itself, visualization can be a relaxation exercise.

This exercise enables you to get in touch with surrounding realities and contact textures such as furniture, walls, foliage, fabrics, sand or even the stones in a babbling brook running over your bare feet. When you work, you are surrounded by some of these real elements as well as imaginary elements. Real elements can be made pertinent by endowing them with other meanings. For example, you can explore the fabric of a real chair as if it were the fabric of a chair from a room with strong memories for you.

To fuel an actor's creative process, the actual scenery can be visually transformed into another room or place and the other actors can likewise be transformed into other people, or even objects, such as trees. The principles of personalization can be used by projecting images from the mind upon other actors as if the other actors are a motion picture screen upon which your mind unreels strongly focused images.

Meaningful places in which significant experiences occurred are excellent choices for this technique tool. You can select a place which you have not seen for a long time, perhaps a place from childhood. Perhaps your choice can be the place in which you are now living. For numerous people, the place in which they live can mean just as much to them as friendships with people—and sometimes, when one considers the satisfying joys of being alone, surrounded by comforting objects of one kind or another, it can mean more.

Gently glide into creating your place by hearing sounds, gathering acoustical information about your place while your eyes are still gently closed. Try not to be concerned with the visual input from the place until you have created the sounds as well as the aromas and temperature. As the images come into your mind in a blurred way, be aware of what you are sitting on; the chair on which you are sitting can be transformed into a tree stump or the edge of a bed. Recollect the texture of the clothes you wore in a certain place and explore those textures without touching the clothes you are wearing. If there was any degree of nakedness in the place, get a sense of that feeling.

This kind of exploration, while the eyes are still lightly closed, will give you a beginning point for establishing a foundation for the remainder of the exercise.

Still sitting, begin to build your stream of images, permitting yourself to enter into the particular consciousness of the images and becoming a part of it. Project your images onto the actual place you are in as you open your eyes. If you sense that something behind you is important, you need not twist around in your chair but permit it to revolve until it is in front of you and what was in front of you gradually diminishes or is moved elsewhere. In visual imagery, the elements of a place can revolve around you like a carousel or be fragmentally created. You can create as many elements of the place as you wish simply by projecting them in front of you, onto other actors and the scenery.

The exercise can be done sitting and then standing, and using variations of sitting, standing, lying down, etc. As you move through the place, have a tactile sense of coming in contact with imaginary people and objects. How do they affect you and shape physical behavior?

Explore the place as you look at it. Where do you set its boundaries and limits? It is necessary to explore so that it does not seem as though you are just listening but are also creating the size. It is not necessary to try to create the complete mood too quickly, but outline the objects, set the time of day or night, get a definite sense of sky, walls or ground.

Begin to work with fragments by knowing you have the imaginary ability to put elements of the place wherever you wish, moving them around until you have established the visuals precisely where you want them. It's not much different from moving a painting on a wall until you find a desired place for it to hang. You can blot out or erase what doesn't stimulate you and make affecting parts stronger and clearer.

What are the thoughts of your action? Relate these thoughts to the people in the scene or in an exercise group. The visuals of a place should be projected and not remain in your mind. Is a person you look at a sharp element in your place and not blurred? Is the person something other than a person? The person can be an object with a particular shape and design—a large bouquet of flowers, a rosebush, a soothing waterfall, a battlefield tank or whatever you wish. At all times, be aware of what you are seeing, touching, smelling and hearing so that the place can have a proper effect on your feelings.

If you sit on the floor, retain a sense of the experience when you get up. If the floor becomes a beach, a green lawn or a bed, maintain the sensation of such places on your legs, back and other parts of the body when you rise and move about. Often there is a strong experience when a place is explored by investigating the floor of a room or an outdoor setting. When you sit in a chair again during the exercise, try to recapture the feeling of the floor or ground.

If you are creating a specific room, the following particulars are useful:

...A room on a set or stage can become like a room you know. Using the room you know for concentrational purposes can trigger you into a scene.

...The actual set can be questioned. Ask yourself if there was a time that you lived in, or visited, a room that is similar to the one in which you are performing. Ask whether something significant happened in the room that might be parallel to the scene. Try not to regard the room in a general way, but be specific about its elements so that you inhabit it with behavior.

...Recheck the room to see that you have created all the sensory realities. Attempt to discover realities which may have been glossed over.

...What are you doing in the room? What is the event and the logic of the event as it might relate to a scene which takes place in a room similar to the one you have chosen?

Clurman believed that the sensory element is constantly going on, but that it takes its usual and most permanent form in the realization of a place and the taking-in of the environment. Actors, he said, who come on stage and start talking to other actors without really finding them, or taking a chair and sitting on it without actually finding it, do not give the illusion of the first time, but seem to be doing things by rote. Inexperienced actors, he felt, tend to regard objects in their environment in an abstract way and do not seek the creative aid inherent in the furnishings and props of a set.

Isolating a single strong element can capture many meanings of a place. For example, if you are working for a place in the evening, locate a star or the moon, technically placing them in a way which will evoke a mood. For a room, the proper mood can be captured by dwelling on one portion of it. In other words, the technical use of a place varies with your need to either create the entire place or just one element of it.

In addition to the power that objects have of their own, you can invest them with the power to move towards you and offer tactile sensations to your body. Let the objects come to you; do not reach for them. If you are dealing with a large object, you can imaginatively permit the entire object or just a part of it to move towards you. Let the object press against your body, be in your hand or be suspended in front of you as it intermittently contacts you. Expand your imagination by exploring fragments of objects as you place them wherever you wish on your body. Using objects in this unconventional manner can have a surprising effect. Preferably, this type of exploration takes place during the latter part of the exercise, but in a scene you may immediately wish to create tactile fragments.

SOUND

Sound, once thought to be weaker than sight, taste or smell, is now regarded as having a sometimes more significant force. The ears are thought to be more sensitive than the eyes because sound waves measuring as little as two-billionths of an inch are capable of putting pressure on the ear drum. Patients, for example, under complete anesthesia have been able to recollect the conversation of surgeons and nurses.

Two opposite sounds, such as a waltz and a firetruck siren, are selected for this exercise. The two sounds should be pleasant and unpleasant, soothing and apprehensive, or in other ways diametrically opposed.

Examples For Sound Choices

symphonic music	forest sounds
rock music	party sounds
surf	cameras clicking
rain on the roof	bird songs
blizzard	hammer sounds
explosion	seagulls
a voice	cat fight sounds
a particular conversation	fog horns
waterfall	thunder
wind howling	country quiet
dentist drill	ambulance sound
sound of kisses	meditational "ohm"
wind chimes	alarm clock

Select an action for each sound. Select a third action for the combination of the two sounds during the final part of the exercise.

As you begin to listen to the first sound, do not twist and turn about to indicate the source of the sound. Let the sound come to you and surround you, unless you are creating a distant sound such as a far-away train whistle. As you create an acoustical environment, try not to keep the sound confined in the head, but listen to the sound with your body. Go with the the sound as your total consciousness reacts to it; capture sound waves with the skin and different parts of the body. Listening to the sound with the entire body can create an unusual tingling sensation. If you use music for one of your choices, avoid any external dancelike movements as the sound circulates within the body.

Explore how low sounds affect the lower regions, whereas mid-sounds affect the chest area and high sounds affect the head. Can you feel a sound somewhere deep inside your body? Put your consciousness into it and go with the sound waves. Let it affect the peripheral nervous system and inner organs. Duplicate the sound with different rhythms; explore the sound sitting, standing and moving, preferably avoiding dancelike movements. Return to the chair, sitting down as you permit the sound to diminish. Still sitting, bring in the second sound, exploring it in the same manner as the initial choice. After you have created and explored the second sound, gradually let the first sound return so that you are creating two sounds with your third action.

In life, there can be a multitude of sounds occurring, but in the final part of this exercise only two meaningful sounds are needed. Let there be a difference in the two sounds: one can be loud and the other soft, or they can alternate between loud and soft; one sound can be near and the other far; one fast and the other slow. Use your imagination to work with unusual combinations. Permit them to overlap and run into one another; feel one sound in the upper part of the body and the other in the lower part; one sound can be stationary in the head while the other travels about. Permit the sounds to compete with each other to create something like a state of indecision or other reactions. Try to get a sense of the sound moving like waves through your arms, legs and other body sections. Smell the sounds. Do the sounds have different colors? Let the sound press on different body parts in the way that it pressed on the eardrums. Can your cheeks, palms, breast, stomach and pelvis become like listening posts? These and other uncommon ways of listening to sound permit you to reach into higher realms of sensitization.

SHOWER/BATH

This exercise is an introduction to the most liberating of Method technique exercises. It deals with the kinetic abundance of energy created by varying temperatures which can agitate the acting instrument to strong behavior. Many respected acting technique teachers (Method and otherwise) mention the behavior that can result from working with cold and hot temperatures even though they may not emphasize the benefits acquired in developing the entire sensorial equipment as outlined in this book.

This exercise, and the next exercises of extreme cold and extreme heat, relate to our largest sense—the sense of touch with its myriad nerve endings over the entire body. It is this sense which is constantly giving us the weather report of our environment, and telling us whether we are cold, hot, dry or wet. The touch sense also lets us know about the rough or soft textures of our clothes. The exercise, therefore, is intended to make you aware of the potential the touch sense has for behavior of either physical or mood sensations. You can do the entire exercise with one action such as "to let myself go with all sensations and feelings," or you may want to have several actions for various stages.

The beginning of the exercise is imaginarily undressing in preparation for a shower or bath. When you remove actual clothing in life, it can take a few seconds. For this exercise, removing imaginary clothes is not to be done in a few seconds; instead you expand each moment of the activity in order to accomplish the necessary exploration as you explore each article of clothing for its complete sensory realities of texture, smell or whatever imaginative exploration you wish to do.

You do not deal with the imaginary articles of clothing by visualizing them in your mind, but by creating them as you did the imaginary objects in previous exercises. This kind of exploration of objects continues throughout the exercise as when you create the shower curtain, tile walls, bathtub, soap, faucets, etc. They are created through sensory contact with imaginary objects.

Contact the realities of the room you are in and be aware of what you are sitting on. You can imaginatively superimpose a robe over your actual clothes—as if your actual clothes did not exist at all. Without touching what you are actually wearing, create the texture of the fabric of the imaginary robe, pajamas or other garments. Create the buttons, and zippers. You can begin the removal of your imaginary clothes, such as shoes and socks, as you are sitting. When you remove a clothing article, do not set it aside quickly, but hold it in your hands and gradually explore its properties and qualities. In this way, tactile sensations are aroused and will grow stronger during the exercises.

When you stand, sense the floor—is it carpeted or tiled? What do the imaginary robe or clothes feel like on your skin? As you begin to remove them, explore the sensation of the material as it comes off your arms and legs. There are certain sensations that occur on the arms and legs when we take off clothes, but they are largely ignored or taken for granted in routine daily undressing. Get a sense of the fabric as it slides off your arms and legs.

There should be no rushing to throw aside an article of clothing or hang it on a hook. You need not feel compelled to explore all the realities of an article, but at least try to accomplish the exploration of one or two realities. As you deal with each article, consider how the exploration is related to the moment-to-moment element in acting. When you complete the undressing, take a moment to stand with a sense of nakedness.

If you are embarrassed or self-conscious about this exercise when you do it in a workshop setting (particularly disrobing and sensing total nakedness), discover how the moment-to-moment technique can help you. Using this technique, you are not rushing a moment, but living in it; rather than being overwhelmed and confused, you are dealing with each moment as it comes along. This involves the same type of concentration you need to overcome tiredness, anxiety or boredom to give a performance you may not want to give.

You now turn your attention to the shower or bathtub. Explore the shower curtain or door before stepping inside the tub or stall. When you step in, create the wall tile with your hands and lean against it, sensing the coolness of the tile on parts of your body. Again, be aware of what your feet are touching. Next, specifically locate the faucets and showerhead, feeling the metal shapes.

This exercise is abundant with overall sensations as you now proceed to explore different water temperatures. You begin by turning the faucets to get a lukewarm temperature, having a specific action for that sensation. You may want, as in life, to test the temperature of the water with your hands, arms, legs and feet before stepping under the spray, or sitting down in the tub of water. Actually it is best to do this exercise first as a shower exercise because of the free exploration it offers; later you can repeat it as a tub exercise without exploring all the imaginary clothes and objects. You can simply sit in a chair as if sitting in a bathtub of lukewarm, very hot or very cold water and be aware of what type of sitting behavior and sensations that experience creates for you.

In the shower, have lukewarm water come from directly overhead, so that you need not reach toward it with the neck and head. Let the water come to you. Where does the water contact you and where is its strongest point of concentration? When the water touches your front, is it different from the back? As you progress, permit the water to come from all around you, as in a jacuzzi. Feel the water jetting up from beneath you as well as from the back and sides. Discover which parts of the body are open to sensation and which are not. Some areas can be locked off, and those areas can be susceptible and vulnerable areas to work with. It is helpful, therefore, to permit the water to get into hidden areas. You need not do many movements of muscles and limbs to arouse sensations in hidden areas.

Create the soap by establishing its weight, odor and shape. As you soap yourself, do not substitute your hand for the soap, but create the space between your hand and your body that the soap ordinarily occupies. After sudsing yourself, slowly turn around and experience the suds being rinsed from your body by jets of water from different directions.

Without contacting the faucets, let the water gradually become extremely cold or extremely hot, exploring each degree of the changing temperature. If the reality of the temperature is strongly intense, avoid resisting it or tensing against it. For example, do not wrap your arms around your torso to warm yourself from the extreme cold. Avoid other contortions, such as doubling-up the body. These types of "acting" antics lessen the truthfulness of sensations.

Allow both your physical and sensitive self to be open to the increasing extreme temperatures even when they feel as if they are passing through you like electrical bolts. The beginning exercises with overall sensations are intended to create tactile behaviors which range from a visible quivering of a cold sensation to a melting feeling of a hot sensation. The exercises might even create a vertigo feeling. In later exercises, you can select choices that create a wide range of sensations, moods and feelings without any physical behavior being highly visible. For extreme cold, it is more useful to create a trembling effect by being open to the sensation and permitting its energy to move up and down the body. A trembling, shuddering effect will give you the extreme behavior needed in a scene in which you are not, of course, taking a shower, but an extreme cold shower choice can agitate your acting instrument to capture the physical dynamics of an emotional state.

Many acting technique teachers value overall sensation exercises because of the physical image they can create in one's acting. They can also be valuable in creating an important physical element, which can often be a deciding factor in casting.

When you work with sensations that seize the body and create strong visible behavior, you are working with a choice to create a behavioral extreme; however, the varying temperatures of this exercise contain innumerable choices for endless types of behavior. It is important that you know how the multiplicity of choices can further your technique in creating organic gesture with the entire body.

Be prepared to discover unexpected behavior. A cold shower for example, can at first be very uncomfortable, even unbearably painful, but during the exercise it may turn into an invigorating experience.

Avoid anchoring your feet to the floor. Create strong jets of water temperatures coming up from beneath your feet. Make sure that the movement which ensues in not a general hopping about; it should capture the meaning of your action for that particular moment. In order to get an overall feeling of extreme cold or heat, it is sometimes necessary to feel it in sensitive areas and then permit it to spread to adjoining areas and eventually to the entire body.

When you have completed the exploration of the first extreme temperature, let it slowly diminish as you return to a lukewarm temperature, experiencing the various temperature degrees during the transition. Is the lukewarm temperature more comforting than it was earlier? Now proceed to the other extreme temperature and explore it.

Both extreme temperatures may be initially unpleasant, as it can be when you plunge into a cold pool or icy ocean or first step into a too-hot bath. But the cold water can become pleasant; the hot water can eventually soothe the nerves and induce deep relaxation.

When you complete the exploration of each extreme temperature, let the water travel with you as you walk. Can you still maintain the strong sensation as you move, walk and sit? With extremely hot temperatures, the room may become like a sauna as you move through hot mists. Be aware of how you can, at times, localize an extreme temperature on the face, chest, legs, etc. In future exercises, particularly in the combinations, you can select localized sensations for behavioral touches. In that event, the experience is a localized sensory one and not an overall sensation. For this exercise, however, remain with the overall sensations and experiment slightly with localized sensations for future reference. Experiment in imaginative ways—such as exploring extreme heat on the upper body and extreme cold on the lower; or cold on one side of the body and hot on the other.

Investigate the feelings you have after taking a shower or bath, as those can be unusally strong sensations. Some people after getting out of a very hot tub can feel their heart beating rapidly and experience a vertigo state. This is an example of finding the many sensations inherent in these introductory overall exercises.

EXTREME COLD/EXTREME HEAT

These exercises do not involve any disrobing or working with imaginary objects. You proceed directly to creating sensations that affect the entire body. These exercises offer the means of getting into deeper layers of emotions and feelings. Most of all, they are exercises which are related to the physical more than the psychological element in acting, which Adler believes to be the more important of the two. These exercises will enable you to create physicalities which will permit both audience and camera to connect with your physical aliveness.

As you develop the technique of using overall experiences to create behavior, you will discover an unceasing variety of sensations to which you can respond. Certain sensations will immediately create a character type, such as a warmhearted person, an icy or frigid individual, someone hot with passion or fired by ambition, a cyclonic personality, a person with chameleon mood changes, or other types with visible physicalities. You will begin to be aware of how a hot, heavy humidity can cause you to be irritable or listless and how cold might invigorate or render you immobile.

Examples of Environmental Conditions Which Create Extreme Cold and Heat

zero-degree cold	wet dampness	sizzling day
hot desert	muggy humidity	sticky heat
freezing snow	fierce winds	sleet and hail
torrential rain	moist sea air	chill

Examples of Less Extreme Overall Sensations

warm breeze	whirlpool	body lotions
spring rain	hot springs	fabrics
jacuzzi	sauna	massage oil
soothing bath	balmy air	warm bed

As you complete your relaxation, let the chair become part of the environment—the chair can be a block of ice or a heavy mass of very hot air. This will aid you in triggering the sensation and also create behavior on the back, buttocks and back of legs. Permit the experience in the chair to shape the way in which you stand and how that is related to your action.

While standing, you probably are able to more thoroughly experience the sensation affecting the entire body. Although it is not necessary to anchor yourself in one place, it is helpful to do minimal walking about for the initial exercises. Too much walking about can cancel out the experience although the eventual goal is to retain the sensation as you sit, stand and move about.

Question the degree to which you are willing to experience the sensation. Let yourself go without the behavior being dancelike. Permit the sensation to affect your fibers, tissues and organs. The body should reveal behavior which captures the action.

After the sensation affects the entire body, localize it on the face, arms or legs so that you can experiment with it in localized areas for future combinations. Localized areas can be those in which you experience sensations at their most intense. The value of experimenting with localizations is to know that you can create a behavioral nuance with a choice in one area and other behavioral nuances in other areas with additional choices.

When you keep a sensation localized on the hands and arms, you develop your skills of organic gesture. Gradually, during the exercise work, you develop the ability to create a new kind of communicative vocabulary with the arms and hands and avoid cliche, verbal gesture. The arms contain excessive energy and by localizing sensations on the arms you convert that energy into imaginative and unconventional gesture.

Even though you sustain an overall sensation, its source may have been a momentary experience such as the sudden shock to the body when plunging into a very cold ocean. A conscious attempt is made to sustain such a momentary experience as an overall choice. Try not to interfere with the sensation when it is occurring strongly by resorting to obvious signals, such as pulling clothes away from your hot, sticky body. The experience will occur more strongly and your sensitivity will be freer if you avoid resisting the sensation or acting out conventionalities of wiping your brow, warming your hands, etc.

As an acting choice, you will have creative revelations as to how a sense of cold can be used for fear, suffering or even exhilaration and how heat can wilt your emotions. An audience or camera will accept your sensorial experience in relationship to a scene when it is done with imaginative and selective technique skill. For a scene that occurs indoors you might use rain, wind or scorching weather to achieve authentic behavior.

Attempt to get a peak experience with your choices so that when they are strong it will be like the surging power of an engine functioning with all cylinders wide open. Work with controlling your choice by permitting it to penetrate into the inner organs and localize it—in the stomach, for example—and then release it and let it spread through the body from the localized area. In this way, you begin to learn how impulses can be channeled through the acting instrument with natural body rhythms.

PERSONAL OBJECT

This is often a misunderstood and misused technique exercise. The following explanation of it will give you the necessary details to use it properly.

Interesting gesture is vital to every actor concerned with refined elements of behavior. This exercise enables you to create imaginative, organic gesture and steers you away from imitative gestures. In a way, it enables you to choreograph your arms and hands. As a creative tool, it is one with which you should be supremely selective. Even the finest actors are sometimes subjected to severe criticism by reviewers who object to any excessive wandering of hands and arms. Well-crafted actors have an awareness of moments when a gesture will add meaning. The gesture can be a sustained ingredient throughout a role or it can highlight a brief moment. You need only study and observe what fine actors do with their hands and arms in order to distinguish between thoughtful gesture and gesture that has an empty essence.

This exercise occupies itself with special meanings related to the sense of touch. Strasberg regarded it highly and his students were sometimes required to devote considerable time to this exercise before progressing to another exercise. He emphasized the exercise because of the personal meanings that it can arouse and the telling emotions that result.

This exercise lays the foundation for further exercises that involve an imaginary object. It is gradually expanded so that you not only relate it to the gestures of arms and hands, but also to a gestural sense of the entire body.

Both animate and inanimate objects can be choices for this exercise. Among animate objects can be a person's hands or lips, or the paw of a pet. When you fragment a person or animal, you still retain a sense of the complete object. Inanimate objects offer a wide range of choices because they can be personal possessions of meaningful value—a ring, diploma, teddy bear, crucifix or Star of David. Explore the object in the same way you explored objects in the beginning exercises. With those exercises, you encountered objects with no particular meaning, but now you have the opportunity to explore objects with emotional significance.

As you complete the relaxation, it is not necessary to see the object in your hand, but with your arms and hands still in a relaxed state, permit the object to be in your hand without grasping it. Permit it to move on the palm and around the fingers before gradually exploring it with your fingertips. Preferably, do not make visual contact with it. Begin by exploring the object only in one hand. Come up with answers about the object as you explore its texture. Simply believe that the object is in your hand and sensorially respond to it. Bring your hands together as you begin to explore the object with both hands, letting the exploration capture the meaning of the action. Let it be a human gesture, capturing some of the inherent meaning which is seen in everyday life when people hold their hands together during a moment of thought, concern, anxiety, desire, etc. Most importantly, conceal any definite attitude with the hand which would convey the object's actual presence; its actual presence must be camouflaged so that the source of expression in the hand is not blatantly perceived. This happens when the exercise is misused.

The fingers, at times, can be somewhat closed; from your point of view, the closed fingers are exploring the object, but an audience will see it as expression. The object is there to be explored in various ways and the technique of artistically camouflaging it is one that needs to be developed if you are to discover that personal objects can be of value to you for capturing meanings.

Attempt to explore the object in the beginning stages of the exercise as if only you and the imaginary object exist. You might select a photograph of someone you care for and hold it to your lips or press it against your body. You may be surprised at the immediate emotion that is aroused. And do not think it strange to use a body part of a person, such as a hand or erotic part.

Proceed to the mobility of the object, which can be adventuresome and fascinating in behavioral results. The object is now moved from one area of the body to another. You move it with your hands and do not permit it to move on its own. Again, camouflage the object and conceal it when the hand or hands are in motion, or when the arm moves to bring the object in contact with a part of the body. There should be no technical disclosure of the imaginary object and what is seen should be motions and movements that are behaviorally graphic.

Bring the object to your stomach, heart or chest, letting the movement and contact capture the meaning of your action. Sense the object affecting the nerve endings in those areas. Permit it to remain in an area and remove the hand which placed it there. The object is now on its own, with a gravity and energy to probe nerve endings. After a moment of body area and object synergy, take the object in hand again and move it to the neck, face or part of the head. We all, in our everyday lives, keep our hands moving from one part of the body to another— touching our mouth at one moment, or cheek, ear, back of neck, stomach or leg at other moments.

There is an accumulative expression that the entire body can derive from the mobile exploration of a personal object. Areas of the body that the personal object contacts can continue to be expressive and ultimately create a behavioral design that involves the head, torso, pelvic area, legs, etc.

Work with rhythms as you move the object. You might keep it on the stomach or chest for a short time and then move it to the head area where you might let it remain for a while before moving it elsewhere. With this exercise, you can accomplish startling, long distance movements by having the object contact different parts of the body as you move it from the head area all the way down to your thighs, knees or feet. This kind of mobility will find rare usage in most roles, but it is useful to do so that you can become daring with the extensive range of the object.

Next, keep the object localized in areas, either with your hands or on its own. On its own, the object can wander over the face area, without spilling over to adjacent areas of the neck or shoulders. Work with it localized in numerous areas to discover which create the strongest responses. The main purpose of this continual mobile investigation is to find areas in which gestural expression can take place, however brief the moment. The use of an object in a scene can emphasize a moment with a gestural highlight. Observe film actors in certain close shots bringing a hand to their head area; and determine if this is a conventional, stale gesture or if the actor is attempting to create a gesture with spontaneous organics.

Become aware of the unconscious gestures that you make throughout the day and also the unconscious gestures of others. These can be part of everyday body language, nervous mannerisms or even conscious efforts to give eloquent meaning as seen in public speakers with a controlled center, who are aware of every little movement.

A human being's hands go everywhere—including hidden areas such as the armpits, into the pockets, behind the back, etc., and the purpose of the exercise is for you to discover how you contact those areas with whatever meaning you wish to create.

WANDERING PERSONAL OBJECT

This is an effective exercise which I have developed in my workshop as a continuation of the personal object exercise. Any of the animate or inanimate objects that you selected for the personal object exercise can be used again as wandering personal object choices. It enables you to flesh out captivating behavioral nuances and to create completely spontaneous energy with an absence of interferences. It allows you to experience a new gestural sense with the body in the way that the personal object exercise created a more imaginative gestural sense with the hands and arms. When it is done with effectiveness, every physical nuance and body gesture communicates specific feelings. It is a tool to permit the acting instrument to function any way you wish, as new fresh impulses are created with physical subtleties. You will discover that it is a reliable means of expressing and physicalizing ideas and meanings.

The exercise deals directly with the body's great tactile organ, the skin. The wandering personal object choice wanders over the skin to evoke visible physical sensations as well as moods which create a stronger presence. It is not only a continuation of the overall exercises but opens up innumerable choices which are not limited to environmental choices. Some actors have discovered that this exercise affects their nerve endings more than overall choices.

As with the personal object, your choices can be the sensual and erotically pleasurable parts of the body. You can select a person's sexual organ, hair, lips, breasts, etc. In painting, this is termed "erotic fragmentation." Compel choices of an erotic nature to explore personal areas about which you may have exploratory reluctance. Let the entire body expose itself to an erotic object and be receptive to it, being particularly mindful that you explore all parts of upper and lower body.

Actors have experienced this exercise in a therapeutic way. One actor revealed that his choice had so affected certain areas that he felt as if he had been Rolfed—a massage technique which dissolves physical and psychological blocks. An actress who got fine sensations with the overall exercises was able to get new body language with the wandering personal object. Another actress permitted her virtuoso voice to emerge from areas where she localized an object—in her pelvis, left rib cage and other areas. An actor was able to create uncouth behavior for the first time as his object choice moved up and down his legs. Many are able to get telling results not easily attained with the overall sensations. The major reason for this is that choices for a wandering personal object have a wider range than environmental conditions that govern the choices for overall sensations.

An auxiliary of this exercise is a wandering object. A wandering object need not have any particular emotional meaning but still can arouse tactile response. Examples of a wandering object are a rose, ice cube, brush, thistle or feather.

Exercise Procedure

Let an object of personal meaning be on an area of your body without placing it there with your hands. Permit it to explore the localized area with its own gravitational energy. At times, the muscles of the area explore the object; the muscles and the object can be synergic as they affect one another. Permit the object to press against the chosen area. Respond to the pressure with the muscles of the area so that the object and area communicate with one another. Whenever the object is localized in an area during the exercise, try to sense what research scientists call skin talk. Sense the conversation of the skin in localized areas with the object. Determine if the conversation between the skin and the object can give you a clue to what is happening deep inside the body in any given area. The object can create interior feelings when the energy of it penetrates into the body while the outer physical behavior is maintained.

Sense the object, but avoid looking at it. Permit the skin to see the object. Naturally, when the object is localized or moving over the face, eye expressions will occur when the sight is affected by its presence. Another important technical detail is to keep the object away from the arms during the beginning work with the exercise. The arms tend to be associated with the hands and the use of the hands in exploring personal objects. Keep the arms totally relaxed during the initial work; later you may permit the object to wander up and down the arms and around the hands, but avoid any impulse to let it become a personal object by touching or holding it with your fingers. A combination challenge for a future exercise would be to include both a wandering personal object and a personal object, getting a gestural sense with two different choices as expressions occur in the hands with a personal object while expressions are occurring elsewhere with the wandering personal object.

Begin to let the object wander out of the localized area and move over the body as if it had a built-in motor. Permit your imagination to maneuver and manipulate it, creating means of transportation for the object to travel over the body, creating physical movements in the areas it contacts.

Permit it to wander with a variety of rhythms. It can move rapidly down the torso, only to move slowly in the pelvic area and regain speed as it travels down one leg or the other. It can stop to explore a localized area which sensitively responds to it and then move again. For a particular type of physical aliveness, allow the object to have its own way as it swiftly moves up, down and around the body.

If the wandering personal object is on the legs, leg movement should occur. Explore it with moving stomach muscles. If the object is on the face, explore it with the cheeks, eyelashes, nose, lips and chin. Let it reside in hidden areas, such as the armpits and crotch.

How does the object fulfill your action? Does it do so with love, hate or anger? Do you enjoy the object or are you indifferent about it making contact with your body? You might experience anger, frustration or repulsion and want to rid yourself of the object, but avoid doing so in order that those feelings may occur at their fullest.

Your initial choices can be the same ones that you made for the personal object exercise, but be mindful, as already mentioned, to make a distinction between the two exercises.

After the beginning experiments, you may wish to use the exercise for creating sensation and mood, without any visible muscular movements. In future combinations, select several wandering personal objects. They may compliment one another, e.g., hands of people you love or who love you. Several objects can be in conflict when one offers pleasure and the other displeasure. Richly use your fantasy and let the objects have a confrontation over possession of your body.

STIMULI EXERCISE

The creation of stimuli is another technique choice that I have developed in my workshop. Stimuli can occur in positive and happy situations as well as in states of fear and anxiety. Shirley MacLaine, upon receiving the Academy Award for *Terms of Endearment*, said she experienced "a physical weakening in the knees," and went on to explain that it was a very unusual sensation since she is also a dancer. Stimuli are extreme reactions to events, encompassing both positive and negative occurrences. If you have had any of the following experiences, then it is a matter of recreating a particular stimulus; if you have not, you can create a sensorial feeling which can approximate a stimulus. With your imagination, you can also create situations which might cause you to breathe rapidly, feel dizzy, etc.

Examples of Stimuli Choices

explosive sensation in head	clammy feet
inability to swallow	perspiring hands
weakness in knees	dry mouth
butterflies in stomach	dizziness
rapid breathing	racing heart
tense feeling in back of neck	blurred vision
shortness of breath	chills
mental fuzziness	tingling in hands
tingling in feet	allergic reactions
shaking with joy	tremors

These are, more or less, the classical stimuli. You should attempt to use your own individual reaction to events which may create a stimulus not on the list. It is also helpful to observe the stimuli reactions that occur in others.

ANIMAL EXERCISE

The origins of this Stanislavski exercise are in the early years of this century, and it has fascinated actors ever since. Its effectiveness has also been employed in numerous growth programs for both children and adults. As a beginning exercise, it helps to release certain inhibitions. Actors, with years of training and experience, arrive at this exercise and discover a new technique tool which can be occasionally used with effectiveness. Some coaches wisely withhold this exercise until the instrument has been more developed. A more developed instrument will often produce infinitely more usable acting behavior.

The exercise is intended to explore both the inner and outer behavior of an animal (mammals, insects, fish, birds or reptiles). The exercise will be useless if you only attempt to copy physical antics and traits of living creatures without entering into their inner life of courage, anxieties, fearlessness, shyness, love and other emotions that humans share with them. You may discover that the inner behavior of an animal can lead to certain creative results which you are seeking. Fascinating results are achieved when simultaneously creating traits of three or four animals. In combination work, a single animal trait can be used with sensorial and other behavioral choices.

The approach to this exercise is first one of observation. Aside from one's pets, other helpful sources are the zoo and nature. Television programs are extremely valuable because of the detailed physicalities presented. Zoo captivity diminishes the natural physicalities of animals and some tend to be active only during feeding time. Nevertheless, we must quickly acknowledge the fact that zoos are contributing towards the future by breeding animals in captivity, since hundreds of species are now extinct and thousands are endangered. If you live in a city near a zoo, you might telephone to find out what time of the day certain animals are more active, aside from their feeding times.

Observation Pointers

...Observe the way in which the animal sits, eats and watches the environment.

...What behavior happens when something captures the animal's attention?

...Probe into the inner impulses that motivate the animal's actions. Why does the animal move and eat in a certain way? How do the eyes mirror the animal's thoughts?

...Capture the clarity of the muscularity in movement and the difference between the human head and the animal's head. Notice how the neck and head tend to be one physical unit. The animal has great power in the head. It fights and grips with the mouth and can break the neck of its victim. The human mouth waits for objects to be brought to it, such as food and drink, whereas the animal slices, tears and attacks with the mouth.

...Note the definite way certain animals hold up their paws, ready for their primary functions. How can you capture the way an animal turns by noting what it does with its paws?

...As you study an animal, attempt to distinguish the animal's traits from your own inner and outer qualities.

...Notice the distribution of the muscular process in the animal's energies. In what way can you control your own muscles to capture what you have seen? In what way does an animal display different kinds of strength in the body and limbs? In this way, you discover that your body can be not just what it is, but what it is not.

The ultimate aim of the exercise is to find something in the behavior of living creatures which you can translate into human terms. As you develop the exercise, you eventually isolate details such as the eyes, walk, limbs, or head for desired expressions. Although most actors first attempt the exercise by doing the entire animal and becoming the animal with complete outer and inner values, that is an optional choice. Michael Chekhov, one of the early practitioners of the exercise, advises the actor to begin with one feature of an animal rather than trying to do the entire animal.

Laura Huxley in her inspirational book, *You Are Not the Target*, suggests that you be alone in a room for an hour and that the animal exercise be done naked with only simple kinds of food that you can eat with your hands. During the hour, attempt to become the animal, eating as the animal eats, thinking, feeling and making noises as the animal does.

The pinpointing of a certain trait of an animal that has a human equivalent is important. For example, pacing in a certain way can be fulfilled by capturing the pace of a tiger. Staring at someone and invading their privacy can be accomplished through the authoritative stare of a lion. A bear can create a nonchalance and looseness in the limbs, as can a chimpanzee or gorilla. A horse can create a body sprint charged with electricity. Comedy elements are created with an ape's manner of picking at the nose and lips. A paw can be used for rubbing the face or head with reflection.

Examples of Animal Combinations

The following are examples of combining animal traits to create behavior. They are intended to guide you in arriving at your own combinations, depending on the action you have selected. The body areas listed after the choices are the areas on your body intended to capture corresponding areas of the animals.

Panther - head   To lash out
Praying mantis - hands
Ostrich - legs

Lion - nose and face   To break out of my
Eagle - eyes   shell and follow
Jaguar - walk   my impulses
Lion - heart
Wolf - back

Flamingo - legs   To behave
Gorilla - arms   outrageously
Mountain Lion - eyes

Giraffe - neck and head   To fight back
Greyback Gorilla - torso, arms
                      and hands
Lion - legs and feet

Monkey - walk   To follow
Horse - prance
Dog - itch

Buffalo - weight   To make contact
Pig - head and breath
Seagull - spine and walk
New Butterfly - wings unfolding

Owl - eyes
Peacock - walk
Bear - physical body
Giraffe - stance
Cat - mannerisms

To take a chance

Horse - legs
Beaver - head
Cat - arms

To bluff my way

Doberman - eyes
Cat - walk and legs
Fish - mouth and lungs

To trap my prey

Cat - head
Bear - torso
Prancing Horse - legs

To set on fire

Other Choices

Octopus - arms
Spider - legs
Ape - extremities
Snake - head
Stork - torso
Duck - feet
Flamingo - legs

Lobster - head and
        legs
Frog - mouth
Fly - feet
Eagle - arms
Monkey - arms

PRIVATE MOMENT EXERCISE

Since you have already experienced the selected private moment in your daily life, all the elements of it have already been established and therefore the exercise is not rehearsed before doing it in a workshop setting. The exercise can also be done in privacy as you investigate the emotional and behavioral details of a private moment and then attempt to keep the quality of a moment as you transfer it to a scene.

GUIDELINES FOR THE PRIVATE MOMENT EVERCISE

...Establish the place in which your private moment occurs. You do this by creating the sensory realities of the place as you visualize it and re-experience it in the workshop.

...The creation of the physical atmosphere of the place can be enhanced by the use of significant objects related to the private moment—clothes, books, photographs, letters, etc.

...Since the exercise is not rehearsed, the involvement with objects is not planned, so that there will be spontaneity as you encounter the objects. Using objects from the past can arouse feelings, as can present-day objects related to a repeated private moment.

...Your own body and thoughts can be a source as you privately express concern about a weight problem or other personal feelings.

...Feelings derived from current private moments have strength because they are connected to your present state of mind and feelings. Examples of this would be preparation for a date with a new love interest, prayer for a loved one who is troubled or ill, or the release of anger on your private surroundings.

...In a workshop setting, the exercise has no purpose if you are aware of those who are observing and watching. A particular kind of concentration is required to create a private moment before an audience.

...The activities in the exercise are not planned. You can select the objects that will involve you in physical activities but the involvement with them during the exercise should be spontaneous. Stanislavski refers to the objects of attention that are necessary within the sphere of public solitude and describes how there must be a surrendering to objects. In the exercise, this occurs when you use objects that have to do with a moment of privacy and become intensely involved with them.

...Try not to refrain from selecting a private moment because of the embarrassment that might occur. If you succeed in making the moment a completely private one, the embarrassment will not occur. A possibly embarrassing private moment can be a supreme test of concentration and faith in yourself and may reap enormous benefits.

...In a workshop, a bright or dark secret revealed through a private moment might astonish the onlookers and/or instructor since its content might be difficult to associate with your everyday essence. But by revealing what no one has ever seen, or can even imagine of you, new areas to be explored will open up.

...Many people will often go to an extreme for privacy— retreating to an attic, desert or mountain; sitting in a parked automobile in order to write a letter, book or play; building a backyard hut in which to meditate or be alone.

...The private moment can be very active or very inactive. One can busily putter about in the attempt to not think about a disturbing incident; one can also sit motionless in depths of depression about an event over which one has no control.

...There are personal happenings in privacy that relate to the struggle to live and develop. It can be gymnastics for the physical self; the sheer enjoyment of prayer or meditation; writing in one's journal; or drilling exercises to improve one's voice and speech, or musical abilities.

...There are people who experience rage in privacy to such an extent that it results in the destruction of objects, e.g., ripping up a telephone book or destroying letters and mementoes of a person with whom a relationship has gone sour. There are tidy perfectionists who rebel over an incident and deliberately scramble the contents of a room only to have self-recrimination about such conduct when the anger subsides and they are faced with the reality of putting everything back in order.

...People talk to other people in fantasy while they are alone, such as verbally assaulting an imaginary person in a rehearsal for a forthcoming encounter. Even defense and prosecuting attorneys imagine the faces of the jury when they prepare speeches.

...There are aspiring actors who, when alone, act all the parts of a movie they have just seen.

...Constructive hobbies can produce satisfaction of varying kinds. For example, U.S. Senate Majority Leader, Howard Baker, wrote a book on photography as the result of the hours of tranquility and release from pressure spent in his photographic dark room.

In conclusion, the private moment can be one that occurred only once, one that has happened a few times, or one that is presently occurring.

AFFECTIVE MEMORY EXERCISE

By working with the many details associated with an affective memory, you may discover that an isolated sensorial experience can trigger and arouse the full emotion of the memory. It enables the actor to produce a strong emotion without the lengthy preparation that is customarily used in the recreation of the details which permit the complete reliving of an emotional moment. I have seen lengthy preparations of as long as forty-five minutes for this exercise with no results. As with procedures in such growth programs as EST, Re-Birthing, Primal Scream and others, an extended length of time can be needed to work oneself up to the desired break-through moment. The wisdom of Adler concerning this exercise is that it would be better to use one's imagination to create what the affective memory seeks to do, but she would also say that even the use of imagination needs some basis of acting truth.

A properly trained and sensitized acting instrument can achieve the equivalent effect of an affective memory by arousing a single sensorial detail. In a scene that I did in one of Strasberg's classes, I created a chest pain, which led to a strong emotional result. Afterwards, Strasberg asked me if I had used an affective memory and I told him I had not. I had gotten such a strong result from a sensory experience that it led Strasberg to believe that I had used an affective memory. The chest pain that I recreated was one that I had at the age of seven when I was ill with life-threatening pleurisy.

GUIDELINES FOR THE AFFECTIVE MEMORY EXERCISE

Selection

Clurman said that emotion is the result of specific memories, the recollection of actual experiences. Strasberg recommended that choices should be experiences that are at least 7 years old, with the best being those that go farther back, even to childhood. He emphasized that recent traumas are to be avoided as they tend to rekindle a current psychological state and can be harmful. Deeply buried experiences, such as those in childhood, contain certain emotions that did not surface but can still be tapped and released. This, of course, can be of enormous therapeutic value and helpful to the strengthening of an actor's emotional instrument. Try not to avoid events that you would rather not touch upon. In professional circumstances you are required to touch all emotions. In the creative professions, even pianists, singers or ballet dancers must perform material which they do not particularly like. Events that have happened during the ups and downs of life experiences are different, even unique, in their content and provide a varied range from which to select affective memories.

Relaxation

In discussions of this exercise, Strasberg often quoted Wordsworth's memorable phrase of "emotion remembered in tranquility." The exercise begins, therefore, with relaxation and not thinking of the exercise.

Setting

The setting need not be interior or exterior, but can go from one to the other. A choice can sometimes cover different locales that are woven into the sequence of the experience.

Prelude

Strasberg advised the actor to create the five minutes before the actual event and concentrate on the final five minutes of it. In the exercise, each of the five minute periods will be of longer duration because of the necessity to explore all the realities of each period. So, find a way of expanding a five minute segment into the longer time period needed for exploration. As a preparation choice for a scene, you can allow yourself a few minutes to recreate the experience of the exercise.

Initial Contact

Gradually begin to have contact with what you see, hear, taste, smell, and touch. What are the sensations of clothing and temperature on the body? Try not to generalize any of this, but make detailed contact as you verbalize and narrate the specifics.

Narrative

Begin to narrate the details as you sit in a chair—the entire exercise is usually done sitting in a chair, an early influence of the Freudian psychoanalytic couch. Verbalizing may be difficult, but an effort has to be made to put the experience into words. You do not, however, concern yourself with merely telling a story, just as you should not be concerned about the emotion being evoked. As the narration occurs, forgotten details will surface and these details can often trigger the desired emotion.

Narrative Contents

...What are the colors, shapes and forms of the place?
...What is the precise nature of the acoustical environment (voices, street noise, screams or laughter)? Describe them specifically—their rhythms, tonalities and volume levels.
...Describe what you are sitting on, what your feet are contacting—carpet, hardwood floor, cement, dirt, sand, etc. Are you wearing shoes? Describe them. Or are you barefooted? All this detailed investigation is necessary as you do not know in advance what detail will trigger a strong surge of emotion.
...What objects are in the place? What objects do you easily remember and what objects are being blocked out?

Concentrate on these objects in an individual way to explore their intrinsic meanings. Touch the imaginary objects and explore them in the way you explored objects in the personal object exercise.

...What tactile sensations does the body experience from the clothes you were wearing in the past event and in what way was the body affected by sensations of cold, heat, breezes, sun or other overall sensations?

...Is your body tensed and frightened, trembling, shocked, in pain, nervous, calm or tingling with exhilaration?

...What are the expressions of the people you see? What are they wearing? What are they saying? What sensations are they having?

...As you sit, describe your body in other positions or motions, as if you were standing and moving. During the other stages of the exercise, you can explore movement.

...Distinguish between this exercise and the place exercise, even if a place can be a mini-affective memory exercise. The place exercise was concerned with the senses and everyday feelings; the affective memory goes beyond that because of its attempt to deal with traumatic experiences which contain the emotional strength needed for exceptionally strong acting moments.

Incorporating Tasks and Activities

As you continue to verbalize, cease working with imaginary objects and begin to work with an actual physical object. It can be a very simple activity of daily life—a comb, pencil, book or even the actual kind of prop that you will use in a scene which may not be related to your affective memory. By using an object that you will be using in a scene during a highly emotional moment, you can get a strong sense of words and feelings fusing with the activity.

Incorporating Dialogue

To get a sense of the direct creative application of this exercise to a scene, you introduce the actual dialogue of a scene when the desired emotion has been aroused. When the exercise is not done in relationship to a scene, this stage can be omitted.

End the exercise when the desired results have been accomplished. Analyze the different stages of the exercise as to what was there and what was not. What else did you discover? Is the emotion stronger, having increased its strength through a time lapse, or has it faded? It will not demand very much psychological insight to determine that there are certain emotional events in your life which have not only conditioned you but will always be with you and creatively useful.

PART III
COMBINATIONS: A
WEALTH OF
NUANCES

Part III

Combinations: A Wealth of Nuances

INTRODUCTION TO COMBINATIONS

The basic technique exercises offer a variety of resources which can be augmented into further creative dimensions. This is accomplished by blending elements from totally different experiences. During this process, you fuse sensorial experiences which have no relationship to each other. This enables you to begin an extension of the instrument as you realize the prodigious capacities of the human sensory system to achieve unlimited orchestral effects. Combinations are based on the time-honored principle of creating new results by inventing new experiences with elements that have never been combined. This combining ingredient is an indispensable part of numerous artistic pursuits. Abstract and expressionist paintings, for example, are ablaze with divergent colors, shapes and lines, but they also exhibit a clearly defined control in the harmonizing of colliding ingredients.

There are popular television serial actors who have created commanding images with a mixture of a physical trait (such as a shrug of a shoulder), rhythmic and tonal vocal qualities, a manner of walking and a specific kind of gesture. The resulting stylistic verve and physical sensuality of such a mixture are gratefully captured by camera lens and appreciated by millions of faithful viewers.

For the actor, it can be of no little consequence to know how to use forces of opposites to hone a new and more viable image. This can be a means to trigger a 180-degree turn in one's sense of a flexible craft. Painters are still inventing new colors, and the actor can do the same.

A desirable approach is to examine and reappraise the components of your talent. During such a process, the components are refined and polished to suit a more effective image. The individual components are then unified in order to determine if the change is effective and desirable. This is a creative and intellectual endeavor with which one can experiment until the desired result is accomplished.

An actor may have dynamics, but there can be power missing in the contrast of elements which contribute to the dynamics. This happens when elements are ineffectively woven together and need to be separated, examined, revitalized with new juices and then put together into a more compelling unit.

The purpose of combinations is for the actor to discover how the mind, the emotions and the physical can merge and influence one another. You should be able to work in all three areas at the same time. The function of combinations can be seen in the early years of a child's life, when he or she begins to put things together in an imaginative, creative way. Combinations allow you to function on several levels of consciousness through unusual concentrational means. The use of combinations in technique development creates dimensional results not easily acquired through singular choices—sharp taste, sunshine, personal object, personalization, etc.

The following are values to consider when working with the technique of combinations.

Quality of the Choices

...Examine every subtle detail of each choice.
...The success of any mixture, as with any fine recipe, is the right amount of this and the right amount of that.
...Create a wedding of choices that may seem improbable in the company of each other.
...Regard the shades and colors of each choice.

Controlling the Choices

...Starting with one choice, let it segue seamlessly into additional choices. Be aware of how they affect one another as well as how they are artistically interdependent.
...Sensitively connect with the elusive internal balance of a challenging combination.
...Be aware of the dramatic twists and turns that occur with choices, their momentary disappearances and the effort required to get them back into the fold.

Rhythms of the Choices

...Regard the mental, physical and emotional choices as members of an orchestra and discover how you, the conductor, create the tonal value desired.

...Select rhythms and melodies that are both soothing and disturbing.

...Let there be polyrhythms. Elvis Presley, for example, created a new popular muscial form by adding blues and revivalist rhythms to hillbilly music.

...As you work with combinations you will discover that you can not just bring different experiences together without giving them careful thought if the combination is to have dramatic logic for the behavioral moment.

COMBINATION EXERCISES

These are the components which will help you with composing combinations.

Inner senses: taste, smell or pain.

Outer senses: sound, or localized tactile sensation, e.g., cold on hands or heat on face.

Overalls: overall sensations affect the nerve endings over the entire body. Typical choices are heat, cold, steam, rain, shower, mist, wind and breeze. The overall should be specifically defined. A breeze, for example, can be gentle, warm or soft; an overall cold can be a cold room or freezing rain.

Place: the visual aspect of a place seems to be the most preferable for combinations, although a sensory reality, such as smell or sound, can be chosen from a place as long as smell or sound is not being used in another part of the combination. This can be, at first, a little confusing, but the examples given provide clarification.

A stimuli choice, personal object, or wandering personal object can also be part of the combinations. These are the abbreviations for the choices:

S—Sense

OA—Overall

PL—Place

PO—Personal Object

WPO—Wandering Personal Object

STI.—Stimuli

Execute combinations in the order suggested. For example, with "2S-OA," the inner sense should be done first, followed by the outer sense and concluding with the overall. In other choices that may not involve an inner sense, such as OA-PO-PL, you still begin with the first choice before proceeding to the other choices. You can actually regard a combination as several exercises. When you add your second choice, you have created a different experience as you will when you add your third, fourth or even fifth choice. Try to analyze the changes that take place as you create each part of the combination until the whole combination has been completed. If you are working with a combination of four or five tasks, allot a little less or a little more than a minute for each task so that you can get the whole combination going for exploration.

Combination Examples

1S - OA	1S - OA - STI.
OA - PL	STI. - 2 PO
3S - OA	STI. - OA
1S - PO	2S - WPO
2S - PL	PL - WPO
OA - PO	2 WPO
2S - PO	OA - PL - WPO
3S - PL	1S - PL - WPO
1S - OA - PL	OA - WPO
OA - PO - PL	1S - PO - WPO
OA - PL - 2 PO	PL - 2 WPO
2S - OA - PO	STI. - WPO
STI. - PL	1S - OA - 2 WPO
2S - STI.	OA - PO - WPO
2 STI.	2S - PL - 2 WPO

The following combinations, created by actors in my workshop, are listed to further clarify the procedure of combinations. They are not intended to be used as formulas for behavior; you should create your own choices.

2S - OA   To rule with power
    Smell - exhaust fumes
    Sound - electric guitar,
           rock music
    OA - cold shower

3S - PL   To flirt
    Taste - honey
    Sound - bells
    Smell - incense
    PL - visual

1S - OA - PL
Smell - rose garden
OA - ocean breeze
PL - visual of a temple

To admire

3S - OA
Taste - shrimp
Pain - in neck
Sound - running brook
OA - soft rain

To keep myself attached
to people

2S - PL
Smell - gasoline fumes
Sound - people at a rally
PL - indoor room

To incite

3S - PL
Taste - satin
* Touch - extreme cold on
chest
* Touch - hot liquid on
crotch
PL - visual

To take a chance

3S - 2PO
Taste - baked fish
Touch - numbness in
hands
Sound - windchime
PO - hat
PO - ball point pen

To find something to do

---

* When a tactile sensation is used for a localized area, it is considered a sense
and not an overall sensation. Any overall sensation, therefore, can be a sense
choice by localizing it.

3S - PL   To laugh at the world
    Taste - clear mint
    Smell - French
           whorehouse perfume
    Sound - New Orleans
           jazz
    PL - Visual of a villa
        overlooking
        Mediterranean Sea
        at sunset

1S - OA - PL   To admire the world
    Taste - chocolate mousse
    OA - sunshine
    PL - visual

2S - OA - PL   To blast
    Taste - baking soda
    Pain - full bladder
    OA - humid heat
    PL - visual of exterior

2S - PL   To go back in time
    Smell - garlic
    Sound - grandfather's
           voice
    PL - basement of
        parent's home

3S - PL   To do whatever I please
    Taste - cherry life saver
    Sound - Jack-in-the-Box
           music
    Touch - sunshine on legs
        and feet
    PL - visual of outside
        setting

1S - PL   To save myself
    Smell - dead animal
    PL - underneath house;
        confined area

3S - PO   To celebrate
  Smell - fresh
              strawberries
  Sound - freeway
  Touch - rain on chest
  PO - a book

2S - PL - OA   To get someone in bed
  Smell - flowers
  Touch - heat on chest
  PL - visual and sound of
          exterior
  OA - mist

2S - PL - OA   To excite someone
  Smell - fragrant incense
  Sound - jazz music
  PL - visual
  OA - hurricane winds

3S - PL   To feign interest
  Taste - Freeze dried
              coffee grounds
  Congestion in head
  Touch - ice water on legs
  PL - visual of exterior

OA - PO   To hide the lie
  OA - meadow breeze
  PO - personal choice

OA - PO   To expose the hidden
  OA - warm mist in bath   person
        after hot shower
  PO - personal choice

3S - 2 PO   To avoid the truth
  Smell - musty
  Sound - sultry whispers
  Pain - in rear
  2 PO - personal choices

3S - OA   To snatch
    Taste - Coca-cola
    Sound - rusty swing
    Touch - spider's web in
          right hand
    OA - red ants

3S - OA   To encourage everyone to
    Taste - cherries   like the world
    Smell - violets
    Sound - ocean
    OA - sunshine

2 STI. - OA   To hold onto my bearings
    STI. - Implosive feeling in
          head
    STI. - Chills up spine
    OA - blizzard

3S - PL - STI.   To console
    Taste - saltwater
    Pain - toothache
    Touch - sun on face and
          torso
    PL - visual
    STI. - rapid heart beat

1S - STI. - 2 PO   To get rid of someone
    Smell - smoke filled room
    STI. - racing heart
    PO - negative
    PO - positive

2S - 2 WPO   To wound
    Touch - fire on bottom of
          feet
    Frozen blood in veins
    and arms
    WPO - fly
    WPO - roach

STI. - OA - WPO   To find my bearings
  STI. - dizziness
  OA - wind
  WPO - a hand

2S - PL - 2 WP0   To discover the truth
  Taste - peppermint
      candy
  Smell - incense
  PL - visual
  WPO - a hand
  WPO - a brush

2S - PL - WPO   To haul over the coals
  Taste - bitter
  Touch - hot sun in eyes
  PL - smell of a place
  WPO - man's face

1S - STI. - WPO   To arouse commotion
  Taste - whiskey
  STI. - stiff feeling in
      neck
  WPO - a knife

1S - STI. - PL   To enlighten
  Sound - chamber music
      in one ear
      telephone ring in
      other ear
  STI. - goose bumps
  PL - visual

PART IV
CHARACTERIZATION

Part IV

Characterization

Inhabiting Characters

In its deepest sense, characterization is the very nature of the actor's craft: it is the gift to inhabit a diverse array of characters with remarkable depiction. A convincing character portrayal, with every nuance conveyed, creates the illusion that an actor is actually being possessed by the character. The joy of acting is discovering the many characters that dwell within you and the thrill of discovering characters within of which you are totally unaware. An actress can discover she can do roles from a femme fatale to an ethereal, stylish woman just as an actor can discover he can do roles from a beefy, propulsive truckdriver to a cool, powerful tycoon.

One of the numerous new movements in acting styles has been towards non-acting, (one of its forms being acting for the camera) in which the performer does not attempt to create a character, but is the character at all times. With this style, the actor doesn't try to become another character but uses his or her personal inner and outer properties to be the character. The actor need never become the character because the actor already is the character. This style is a spinoff from the time when the Hollywood image makers refused to permit their contract players to be anything but themselves since that was what the box office demanded. Some recent and contemporary actors still carry on this tradition with noteworthy success, slightly changing nuances from role to role. They add slight behavioral touches with each new role which enable them to be more than a mere personality. For a personality actor, character touches would be superfluous to an established image.

Actors who create characters belong to different categories. Some of them are:

- Deeply intuitive actors who get right inside their characters.
- Actors who have sensitive qualities which can inhabit a character.
- Actors who do not want to have a fixed role and be typed.

Having the available means to create characters enables you to deal with standard material which is often fluff or exploitative, giving it more substance than it actually has. Certain actors can give class to a film. Film studios, in the thirties and forties, hired top British actors to do small character roles, because they were able to create memorable cameo gems, often taking a nothing role and turning it into a remarkable one.

Fleshing Out a Character

The distinctive physical features that an actor wishes

to convey are qualities that will capture interest. The entire map of the body provides areas with which to convey physiognomical features of a character. The creative perception of the thoughtful actor does not rely on mannerisms which are stale signals—the verbal use of the arms, pelvic perambulations, muscular knots in the forehead, etc. The creative actor seeks organic impulses which result in fresh and spontaneous behavior. Some actors will use a person they know as a model, getting under the skin of that person to capture authentic behavior. For films, since the head area is the one most noticed, the actor should be creatively selective. Film audiences are very sophisticated in their observations of features that are not run-of-the-mill facial expressions.

Numerous subtle details can be involved in creating a character and a fine actor will make sure that they evolve into something that is not studied, but real. Upon deciding the type of character to create, you should begin to think in terms of how the character should sit down—bang down in a chair, flop in it, or sit on the edge. Begin to visualize how the character stands, and shifts the body's weight; the way the character moves, or makes revealing gestures with the head or hands. How does the character enter a room? Does the character storm in or creep in? How does the character pick up a book or drink, or read a newspaper? These are just a few of the elements that help to physicalize a character and give it palpable interest. A number of these elements will take place automatically, but they need to be constantly reinvestigated. Physical qualities need not be especially complex to create captivating features. An indelible character can be created with simple, vivid touches—a way of walking, or a slight nuance in the head and shoulder area.

Where is the character's center? From which part of the body does the energy seem to flow the most? A study of the chakras in Far Eastern beliefs can offer significant clues. By finding centers, the actor inhabits a deep source in the character and tellingly relates to the environment.

Rhythm and tempo are important elements in physicalizing a character. An outer calm can be accompanied by an inner anxiousness or impatience and the contrasts will create a particular kind of rhythm. Whether or not contrasting rhythms exist, it is important to find the character's rhythm. The inner rhythm will, in turn, be heard in the character's verbal life and give it unusual spirit.

Dissolving Your Identity

Discovering the mental characteristics of a character is not an intellectual matter. Knowing about the past, present and future of the character will help you to arrive at choices, but you must resist being overly intellectual. It is important to investigate the way in which your own mental makeup can improperly influence a character. Insecurities, self-consciousness, shyness or self-doubts can maintain a strong hold, and permitting any of these feelings to enter a performance is to remain the actor and not enter into the mental life of the character. For some, acting allows personal problems to be left behind, and they are thankful for the complete escape that is afforded by dissolving their identity in order to completely create another. Some actors successfully personalize the problems they share with a character.

What is the character's mental awareness? Is it an awareness which is hidden or revealed to others? Is the body liked or disliked by the character? Does the character feel insecure because of a complexion problem, unusual height or weight, or even the way an arm dangles from having been broken several times while very young? These are all personal concerns that an actor can have, and can choose, if it is dramatically suitable, to create mental character traits. Adler says this is personalizing things about yourself which can suit the character.

Clurman suggested something very useful for actors who inhibit themselves. He suggested that a way of curing this defect is to take a negative element and make it positive. When one plays fear or timidity, and has difficulty in self-expression, the actor can turn the negative into a positive element by being articulate about inarticulateness. The negative is transformed into a terrific desire to speak, such as a child struggling to pronounce words in order to be understood.

Characteristics of the mind often have nothing to do with physical characteristics. We have all seen people with unusually high intelligence who have a sluggish and uncoordinated physicality—feet dragging, arms hanging listlessly, head and shoulders drooping. Conversely, there is the type who, being aware of lacking intellectual gifts, may cultivate an outward behavior to capture the demeanor of an intellectual.

The Psychological Pants of a Role

Having the ability to transform oneself into another person is the secret of interpretation. An actor's own personality is the source of physical and mental differences, as well as psychological differences. Some actors uncover the psychological (or emotional) state of their characters by first finding physical traits. This is what is termed working from the outside and then going inwards. By finding certain physical traits, inner values are eventually uncovered as you discover the psychological reasons underlying the physical behavior of your character.

Clinically, human beings are classified as belonging to one of four basic psychological types. The great Swiss psychoanalyst, Carl Jung, postulated that we experience the world in four ways: sensation, thinking, feeling and intuition, but we do not belong exclusively to one of these types since we have the capacity for any of them. These are the contradictions in a character which give a role its human inconsistencies, its inner state of flux. These psychological values add rich dimensions to a role, bringing it alive with an inner essence.

The psychological life of the character already exists and in order to get an image of the true inner core, superficial layers often need to be removed. There are actors who have the gift of becoming psychologically possessed by their characters. They have such immediate insight that a character unfolds immediately. Such actors permit a character to take over and inhabit their emotional acting instruments.

Finishing Touches

Even after you have exhausted all possibilities in creating a character and have put them all together, still seek those final touches which will complete your search. Once you have the sense of a character's truth, you can then dress it with the certainty that the outer garments and accessories will fit. Sometimes many touches will be tried and eventually the right one will be found.

The manner in which an actor uses objects can be revealing. An actor is constantly encountering objects which can be used to convey a character touch. Any actor who neglects physical activities with objects as a way of conveying values is not using the directorial imagination that actors possess.

CHARACTERIZATION EXERCISE

The basic procedure for the characterization exercise is as follows:
- Select a character type.
- Choose a suitable action for the type.
- Select a choice, or choices, to create the type for the head (including the neck if you wish) and the facial areas. Select choices for the remainder of the body, i.e., from the neck down.

By this process of selection, you learn that the technical understanding involved in creating one character type is the same understanding that you use in creating all character types.

Although there are numerous examples given on the following pages, it is preferable that you refer to them as suggestions only. As you will note, there is a wide range of character types listed in addition to actions and choices for them, but it is more adventuresome to arrive at your own.

You may wish to use more than one choice to capture facial expressions and head traits. These choices ought to differ from those used to create body traits of movement, gestural use of the arms and hands, postural and torso significances, the walk, etc. At times, however, you may want to use a choice for both the head and body areas, such as an overall sensation, although each area can have other individual traits.

It can be helpful to select an actual object which you feel might be appropriate for the type—an ornate or long cigarette holder, a stethoscope, an attache case, a shorthand pad, a fancy cigar, a string of pearls, a gold top cane or a lengthy chiffon scarf.

For this exercise, it is helpful and illuminating to start with yourself. How do you type yourself? How do others type you? What specific traits do you have that are manifestations of your particular type? Observe others whom you have typed and specify their particular traits.

Be mindful of making choices that will capture the spirit of the character—both the inner and outer life. A character type is not completely created unless you have given thought to voice and speech traits. Vocal characterization choices can be beneficial for attaining more interesting qualities in a voice. Among uninteresting vocal qualities are flatness, lack of energy, a voice rooted in nasal areas of the head, a lack of sufficient resonance in areas of the head and chest or other deficiencies in tonal quality, projection or rhythm. I have often been astonished with the vocal changes realized by some of my students by the use of vocal characterization choices. Choices for vocal characterizations are listed in the example section.

Any particular type can be created in innumerable ways and to different degrees. For example, a shy character type with obvious traits might not be suitable for a shy character whose traits are not easily seen, or are covered up. For whatever reason, many of us have had the experience of not being aware of certain characteristics of a person until someone else mentioned them. We then begin to observe the root cause of traits with which we have been acquainted, but have not analyzed.

Some people can alternate between one type and another which involves the use of choices for a second or third character type.

Character Types

PLACID	KIND	JOYLESS
AGGRESSIVE	IRRITABLE	PERFECTIONIST
MELANCHOLIC	MEAN	HOT TEMPERED
DEPRESSIVE	BORED	RUDE
ARROGANT	MISERLY	LAZY
EFFERVESCENT	PRYING	COY
EGOCENTRIC	DISORDERLY	INSECURE
BLASE	FASTIDIOUS	ALERT
VINDICTIVE	SAD	INTROVERT
DOMINEERING	UNTIDY	POSSESSIVE
DESTRUCTIVE	HAPPY	ECCENTRIC
GIVING	UNHAPPY	VAIN
INTIMIDATING	FRETFUL	BASTARD
INDECISIVE	WITHDRAWN	BITCH
SLOW-WITTED	EXCITABLE	SENSUALIST
SUBMISSIVE	HUMBLE	BOASTFUL
SHY	ZANY	BOSSY
PLAYFUL	WORRISOME	NARCISSISTIC
UNSELFISH	CONFUSED	ADAMANT
PETTY	SURLY	SUBSERVIENT
PROUD	MOROSE	OBNOXIOUS
EXTRAVERT	DECEITFUL	GLUTTONOUS
NERVOUS	PERSEVERING	FRIENDLY
APPREHENSIVE	POLITE	REGAL
FEARFUL	SARCASTIC	HEDONIST
CONFIDENT	HUMORLESS	PETULANT
RETARDED	PURPOSEFUL	MORONIC
HAPPY	FLIPPY-ZANY	SELF-ASSURED
SENSITIVE	INGRATIATING	PLAYFUL
INSENSITIVE	CHARMING	SPIRITUAL
LONELY	EXCITABLE	INFANTILE
INSISTENT	TIMID	PIOUS
CHILDLIKE	WISE	SOCIABLE
SELF-CENTERED	MENACING	EFFUSIVE

Typical Actions of Character Types

Kind	To brighten the atmosphere
Depressed	To find protection
Vindictive	To mock everyone
Decisive	To make them understand
Withdrawn	To learn how to connect with people
Confident	To maintain my dignity
Miserly	To get all I can
Surly	To keep things my way
Sarcastic	To put down
Narcissistic	To capture attention
Sensualist	To get someone in bed
Shy	To shut out the world
Nervous	To be on guard against
Egocentric	To shock
Bossy	To dominate everything about me
Confused	To figure out
Unhappy	To seek help
Morose	To reject everything of possible interest
Aggressive	To make as much connection as I can
Effervescent	To get on the good side of everyone
Indecisive	To pull myself together
Extraverted	To claim my position
Perfectionist	To put everything in order
Subservient	To submit
Boastful	To get their attention
Lazy	To avoid doing anything
Persevering	To want to know more

Characterization Exercise Examples

TYPE	HEAD AREA	BODY AREA
Excitable	Bubbles in head	Rapid heart beat
	Warm breeze on face	Itchy hands
		Ants on legs
Sarcastic	Sickening sweet perfume	Cold wind
	Eye pain irritation	Tightness of muscles in small of back
Timid	Confectioner's sugar	Sense of hummingbirds on knees, toes and elbows
Wise	Smell - spring dirt	Cowbell on thighs
	Visual of a place	Personal Object - a hand

TYPE	HEAD AREA	BODY AREA
Menacing	Steam on head	Steam
		Rapid breathing
		Butterflies in stomach
Perfectionist	Cool breeze	Sound running through body
Gluttonous	Dry mouth	Growling stomach
	Food smells	
Purposeful	Cobra-like head movement	Wind
Bitchy	Sound of mynah bird	Heat
Insistent	Dry mouth	Perspiring hands
Zany	Bubbles in head	Sensation of roller coaster
	Feathers stroking face	

TYPE	HEAD AREA	BODY AREA
Arrogant	Smell of diesel fumes	Feathers on back of legs
	Sound - barroom noise	Pins in chest
Confident	Bubbles in head	Rapid heart beat
	Taste of chocolate	Itchy feet
	Cold on back of neck	Intermittent body numbness
Moronic	Frozen tongue	Heavy burlap sand bag on back
	Electric shock	Sense of muddy field
		Sporadic electric shocks in arms, torso
Extraverted	Cool breeze inside head and throat and going out of those areas	Sparklers inside chest
		Steam on torso, shoulders, arms, hands
		Hot jet springs on bottom half - waist down

TYPE	HEAD AREA	BODY AREA
Self-assured	Wind into face	Wooden boat deck under feet
	Varying temperatures	Body immersed in cool water
	Sound - song	
Miserly	Smell of skunk	Sharp pain in right hip
Perfectionist	Taste of lemon in eyes	Taste of lemon in legs
	Sound of ocean on back of neck	Sound of gong in arms
		Steam
Eccentric	Taste - Mt. Dew Soda	Wet suit on body
	Breeze on face	Warmth in leg and torso
Loner	Numbness between eyes	Thick humid air on body
	Visual of a place	Warmth in crotch
		Smoke in bottom third of lungs

TYPE	HEAD AREA	BODY AREA
Playful	Heat on face	Butterflies in spine
	Sound - marimba music	Splinter on bottom of right foot
Depressive	Taste of vinegar in back of throat	Nausea in stomach
	Headache	
Sarcastic	Jet stream air	Ice cubes localized on testicles
	Sound of splashing water	
Insecure	Steam in nose and throat	Sound of telephone busy signal
		Overall cool air from air conditioner
Vindictive	Pain in teeth	Sound of water dripping through body
	Sound of water dripping	
		Heat lamp on chest
		Itchy fingers

TYPE	HEAD AREA	BODY AREA
Infantile	Buzzing fly inside head	Charm bracelet wandering on body
	Head suspended on pin	Physical fatigue following Aerobic workout

Vocal Characterization Examples

HEAD AREA

Sunshine in head	Pain in teeth
Inflamed sinus	Stiffness in jaws
Stuffed nasal passages	Tickle in nose
Pain in eyes	Cold nose
Frozen tongue	Plugged sinuses
Icy lips	Steam in head
Numbed tongue	Thick liquid in head cavities

THROAT AREA

Frozen vocal nodes

Strep throat

Flute reed in throat

Thick liquid in throat

Bouquet of beer in throat

Whistle in throat

Large ball bearings in back of throat

Lead weights hanging from esophagus

Thorn travelling up and down the esophagus

TORSO AREA

Steam

Hot air

Warmth

Bronchial congestion

Sore lungs

Water dripping down from throat

Hot spicy mint sauce

Indigestion

Heartache

Wind

Bubbles

Sparklers in the chest

Sensation from the chest channeled to top of head

PART V
THE ROLE

Part V

The Role

First Encounter with the Script

Creating a role begins with reading the script when there should be that feeling of coming to the script for the first time. The content of a role is found by seeking those clues that will lead to the choices upon which a full interpretation will depend. By probing and questioning, the actor gets into real involvement with the script. Clurman and Adler are both in agreement that each line of a script is to be investigated, analyzed and completely understood.

As you dissect a script, major questions will rush forward:

...What sense do you receive from the script? For example, if you get a sense of turbulence in the situations and characters, decide what elements in the script have produced this and what it means.

...What is the script about from the standpoint of your

character and how does your character contribute to it? ...What actions can you immediately come up with? You begin to build a character when you formulate a dozen or so actions. Later you can be selective about arriving at the main actions for your role, selecting just a few from the many you have already formulated. Your major actions, of course, should give you a springboard for creating the behavior needed for the entire role.

Since you will find no more eloquent and inspirational advice for analyzing a script, dwell deeply upon the following words of Harold Clurman. I heard them spoken during one of his frequent dynamic moments in his acting workshop and they remain seared in my memory whenever I coach or direct actors.

"You will not be able to play parts well unless you begin to analyze. Your growth as an actor depends on your ability not to get onstage and play well, but to sit down and analyze a part. You must sit down as if you are the director. You will be Elia Kazan telling Franchot Tone what to do. Tell him what to play, why it should be played that way, what is the play's spine and what place in the script has the entire conception of the role. Do it very concretely. It is the director who is the architect; he has the plan. An actor can do the same by listening to each line, so when he acts it well, or badly, at least there is logic and clarity. If he plays it badly at least the audience will see the meaning of what he does. Even if the actor expresses it crudely, at least he is doing the logic of the role and the audience may say that the actor is not right for the role, but at least they see a logic in what the actor is doing and thereby develop a deep interest. You will miss the target until you have the ability to sit down and analyze a role. If you cannot do this, you cannot be good. Even if you have emotion, it will mean nothing. You are like many actors in the American theater who have talent, personality, voice, etc., but you are not good because you cannot think through a role."

Mapping the Course

The priority in script analysis is identifying and interpreting the sections. In film scripts, each scene can be a section; in a play, there will be numerous sections in each act, one following the other without the kind of disruption that exists in film scripts.

Mastering the ability to break a script down into sections enables you to find the intentions with which a character is concerned. You can analyze the script with pin-point precision by knowing the line of dialogue that begins a section and the line on which the section begins to diminish or abruptly ends. Sections can be of varying lengths since an intention can be fulfilled in a very short time, or over a considerable period. In either case, when the intention of a section has been fulfilled, or unfulfilled, it is the signal for the beginning of a new section. In this manner, you begin to have an internal comprehension of the material and a reliable way of authenticating it.

In Adler's script analysis classes, she emphasizes that a script comes to you from another place and that your job is to absorb it into your psyche. In working for sections, or sequence as she calls it, try to give the initial section the most importance and let it lead you into all the sections that follow.

By developing the ability to break down a script into sections, you will avoid the pitfall of acting in a general way and be able to understand the meaning of every moment. Being able to analyze a script can be a saving grace since you cannot expect or hope that the director will always do it for you. Film directors, in particular, are often more concerned with technical matters and have little time for the actor's creative process. The film director expects the actor to have analyzed a script for its intentions and thereby be able to immediately deal with any portion of the shooting schedule. Portions of the script will always be shot out of sequence, but the actor need not feel displaced if the various sections have been given their individual identity.

Strasberg emphasized that the blocking out of sections is an element present in all fine acting, consciously or unconsciously. The blocking out of sections offers you the liberty and freedom to know that when you comprehend the meaning of a moment, you can then reach beyond it and create the experience, sensations and life needed for the role.

The stage actor gains an inner life and continuity by blocking out sections. A continuous movement is present as the actor interweaves the performance, flowing in and out of sections, creating the moment-to-moment life of the role. When you have seamlessly woven all of the sections of the role and have delineated the beginning and end of each section, you have imposed an order on the material and given it a form into which your acting energies can enter.

For the screen actor, sections are of equal value, even if the role does not have the continuous kind of movement of stage acting. The screen actor performs in short periods of time, broken up into bits and pieces. Knowing the precise meaning of a section gives the film actor the facility to bridge the time lapses that occur between working days. By knowing the precise meaning of a section, both the stage and film actor will also be aware of the line or lines of dialogue at which the action will be at its strongest.

Clurman said that the lines of a script dictate the sections, whether the sections have five lines or fifty. Sections are determined by receiving impressions of new and different events happening in the dialogue. These impressions will reveal what your character is trying to achieve and what your character wants to achieve by saying the words written for any particular section.

Composing a cue sheet helps to identify the lines of dialogue which begin sections. Examples of such cue sheets (or scene breakdowns as they are sometimes called) can be found in the appendix.

When planning your role's "road map," be open to revisions and rearrangements as you deal with basic rudiments. The homework you do with sections requires discipline, but it rewards you with a more dynamic vision of your role and what you can do with it. Aside from that, there is the professional respect you gain as a performer who can succinctly explain the creative content of your acting. Following scene work, Strasberg always required an actor to explain his work by asking, "What did you try to do?". This helped him to tell actors to what degree their intentions were accomplished.

Dialogue Entering Your Consciousness

As you blueprint a script, automatic vibrations occur which include memorization of the dialogue. Numerous actors memorize simply by studying a script for its content. Involvement with the internal structure permits dialogue to enter your consciousness more easily, and helps you to thereby avoid the verbal trap that can occur when memorization takes place before the analytical process.

Truth in Dialogue

Your concern is not with the verbal which belongs to the writer; your concern is with the nonverbal. There is a close relationship to the author's dialogue when your voice and speech are colored by your own sensations. The author does not conceive his work with words. There first passes through him various impulses and sensations. The words on paper are the final product of his creative process.

The words and sounds are the final product of the actor's process, not the beginning as in verbal acting. Verbal acting is often rooted in the standard type of acting training in which words are not spontaneously conceived in the actor's instrument and lack an individuality.

One of the most illustrative examples of the objectionable in conventional acting occurs when the actor delivers lines with preconceived meanings. In conventional acting, a verbal approach is so ingrained that whatever occurs in performance has been determined before the actor reads the script for the first time. With a deeply ingrained verbal approach, it is impossible to conceive a role with the freshness that is present when the senses are alive. Verbal emphasis and organic use of self are incompatible. Verbal acting is the tyranny of the mind over the organic use of the acting instrument.

Comparsion of *Nonverbal and Verbal* Acting Processes

NONVERBAL ACTING	VERBAL ACTING
The words capture realities and meanings.	The words are rhetorical. This does not imply that the rhetorical actor is insensitive. On the contrary, a high artistic sensitivity may exist, but not be used to capture verbal realities.
Words are secondary to thoughts, sensations and feelings.	Words are of prime importance.
There is no verbal mask or damming up of impulses. What results is voice and speech with a personal reality.	Verbal actors tend to hide behind a verbal mask, not achieving the personal speech that occurs when impulses are permitted to lead the way to words. The sound of the words only suggests the actual experience.
The verbal utterance captures the reality of everyday conversation which makes the nonverbal actor very human.	The fusion of feeling and words does not occur organically and there is a preoccupation with surface values.

NONVERBAL ACTING	VERBAL ACTING
The actor is not concerned with the way the words will sound. There is a trust that the words will have meanings without consciously being frozen in time.	The words flow with preconceived decorations and rigid ideas about how the words should sound.
The actor is close to the character when unaware of what line is next.	The verbal actor is concerned about the character's next line and plans the way it should be said.
There is human sound with verbal spontaneity. The words emerge differently each time, but always have a proper meaning of the moment. The actor is not a verbal trap victim.	The actor is caught in a verbal trap, knowing how the words are going to sound.
The actor creates the reality of the circumstances and environment and permits that reality to condition the words and sounds.	Since everything is preconceived, there is little reality. There can be vivid and impressive emotion, but little unconventional reality.
Expression is free and spontaneous because the reality created determines the sound. The actor conveys a feeling of saying words that never existed.	True powers of creative expression are not entirely realized. Those powers are lessened when the verbal line is planned.

NONVERBAL ACTING	VERBAL ACTING
The actor's concern with the reality of the words prevents a verbal pattern.	A strong verbal pattern is present when the actor is preoccupied with the literal significance of the words.

The very essence of acting is the recreation of life, not the imitation of it. By imitating life, verbal acting automatically excludes an organic fusion of emotion, sound and meaning. In many universities, focus is placed on ensuring that the actor has the equipment to meet the demands of the dramatic power of classical dialogue. Instructors emphasize securely focused vowel tones and the development of a voice with the range and power capable of making compelling sounds. Many fine American actors have benefited from this training by having their range extended. When the American theater was still producing classics on Broadway, cultivated speech was mandatory. Nowadays, most Broadway productions require an urban, vernacular way of speaking. Contemporary playwrights write with the knowledge that 70% of communication is nonverbal. Their plays often use nonverbal behavior, rather than abundant dialogue, to provide the essential information.

Letting the Role Take Flight

During the years that techniques for modern acting have been developing, numerous theories have been advanced with respect to the elements with which the actor must be concerned when approaching a role. When these theories are taken together, the actor is confronted with an overwhelming compilation of concerns and obligations. The actor, however, should not get too bogged down with theorizing, as that would constipate an actor's true purpose which is to act and not theorize. The following are additional elements upon which you should dwell during preliminary analysis of a role.

Shaping Behavior

The way in which an actor conveys a character is through the character's behavior. What a character does, of course, conveys a character's way of doing things. A personality actor never needs to convey qualities that are not natural qualities since the creation of character detail would be superfluous for that type of acting.

The finest acting has to do with the creation of behavior. This focus enables you to become a human being, a living character, and not just an actor.

Adler suggests that a way to test your character, while giving it shape, is to put your character in situations away from the script, such as contexts that have to do with money, recreation, work and family.

Glowing Moments with Inventive Details

Numerous fine actors work interminably on their roles in the attempt to find captivating details which will add dimensions to their performance. They experience a meaningful give-and-take process: an actor shapes the role and the role, in turn, shapes the actor to the point of transformation.

You study a script to find out what your character is

trying to accomplish at every moment, both inwardly and outwardly. Some actors will select many obstacles and problems as a way of reaching the precise feelings they need and then they will begin to discard some. When faced with an imposing array of details, it can be a small detail that can get a scene going for you.

Exploring Your Character

Your emotional research of a role involves finding clues which will reveal something about the psychological type of the character. Actors have private means of conducting this kind of investigation: some visit the locales which their characters inhabit; others will experiment with makeup; and some even find it helpful to dress up as their characters when preparing a role. Actors can undertake all of these types of investigations, and some actors find this a more creatively fulfilling period than the performance itself!

Being Right on the Mark

Your job is to make points about a scene. If you are not right on the mark, whether it is the beginning, middle or end of a scene, then some part of the scene has been slurred. It is necessary to find out what you want to convey in a scene. For example, you can convey something in terms of characterization by finding a way to walk or speak.

Living in Your Environment

An arousal occurs when the actor imagines the type of environment in which a character dwells and moves. You investigate your character's environment by finding out what has been placed there by your character and how you use it. Adler suggests that when you work on an actual set, you can approach it by walking around it so that you begin to energize your "stage legs." You need not walk around the set as the character, you can walk around it as yourself, thinking about whatever you wish to think about. You can also be thinking about nothing at all.

The director usually has the scenic plan of movements and handling of props, but you can always find insightful ways to immeasurably add to a scene by fulfilling directorial requests with additional dimensions. A director may stage a scene by having two characters sitting at a table; you can find elements in a table scene which can enhance the situation such as revealing hidden complexities by the way you move a chair.

Not Starting from Point Zero

A scene does not simply begin from point zero; the events that precede a scene are just as important as the scene itself. It is up to you, and you alone, to find out what the scene is about by analyzing each word, each line.

What is the circumstance of the scene?

How has it come about? If there is something about the scene that relates to a past event, you need to conjure up images of that event.

Who is responsible for the circumstance?

Does the circumstance bring you together with other characters or separate you from them?

Who controls the circumstance?

How does the scene begin? You find out how a scene begins by going over what happened in a preceding scene. This will tell you if the following scene should begin with a sigh of relief, a note of fury or complete determination.

Every moment in a script, as with every moment in life, is preceded by a circumstance. The present moment of any scene is itself the given circumstance for the next scene. A thoughtful actor will give regard to this kind of sequence.

Numerous actors had already embarked upon illustrious careers before being accepted as members of the Actors Studio. Strasberg was completely satisfied if he was able to instill a deeper, more incisive logic in their acting. He often referred to the logic of character and pointed out what would be illogical for a character to do.

Human logical functioning enables us to correct ourselves when we are not functioning properly. In acting, it is important to be aware if you tend to be more concerned with a verbal logic and to give a backseat to emotional logic. Very interesting acting is not created when one goes with the apparent logic of a scene. Original and intriguing values are attained when the actor attempts to transgress the obvious logic. In order to accomplish this, there should be a creative involvement with both inner and outer values, as well as with the obstacles to a character's intentions.

The meaning of a scene is created through logic. There is a logic for awakening with a hangover and a logic for springing out of bed with a burst of energy. There is a logic for how a character spends time before a mirror, and performs a myriad of rituals before leaving home; there is a logic for going out into a bright sunny day and another logic for facing biting winds. These may be basic examples, but there are unskilled actors who are incapable of creating simple, logical truths. For example, there is a certain logic for how a character would sit down in a 15th century antique chair and another logic for flopping down into a modern chair. Even characters who are oblivious to the kind of chair they are sitting on have their peculiar logic.

Every Script Needs to Be Described

Any actor realizes that the acting instrument must describe what is taking place in a situation. The actor can opt for conventional choices which can be interesting. On a more creative level, an actor will probe to find elements that will create imaginative human behavior to describe a situation in an unconventional way.

How, then, do you go about describing the situations of a script with alive, unconventional behavior? Once the actions and behavioral choices have been determined, you should then be ready to make a total commitment, and submit yourself not to words, but to the situation.

Nurturing a respect for a script demands hours of work—sometimes entire days or weeks. When you work at home, you create a fertile territory which you can transplant to any set, stage or location. While working alone, create imaginary territories of the script by visualizing the types of people and scenery which will occupy acting spaces. When entering into the actual rehearsal or filming environment, your nerves and sensitivities will begin to be charged as you call upon what you have already richly visualized while working alone.

Much solitary work is nonverbal. You should develop strong trust in your ability to work without words. Entire scenes can be tackled without words through actions and choices. During this process, you are not concerned with how a role will be acted but with the nonverbal elements which create the aliveness desired. At the same time, you should develop an awareness of what the other characters are saying, and of the nonverbal meanings behind their

words as well. Adler says that this will be helpful when
beginning a scene, because you can already imagine what
has been said to you and then when you go to the lines
of the script, you can begin your reaction to what you
have imaginarily heard.

Inner Detail/Outer Detail

Actors sometimes explain their approach to a role as
starting from the outside (often overdoing it) and then
gradually going inside for final exploration. There are also
actors who use a reverse approach, working out the inner
detail before adding the outer, or the "overcoat," as it is
sometimes called. Still, a third group will work on both
simultaneously, as inner exploration gives immediate rise
to outer details.

The strengthening of the inner state of the actor is
emphasized by most acting teachers, but there are teachers
who are more concerned with visceral and vocal power;
both are of value. Too much concern with the inner process
can be detrimental and result in what has been called
bottled-up emotions.

The inner and outer process is perhaps more noticeable
in the creation of a play than in film work which is not
concerned with a long, drawn-out acting process, but only
with the results needed from a day's shooting. In the
rehearsal of a stage play, procedures will vary: good actors
and good directors are aware that although everyone is
working differently, they are still all concerned with a
common goal during the deepening rehearsal period.

Top actors admit that if their jobs depended on what
they reveal during early rehearsals, they would be
replaced, and that it is only the director's awareness of
their process that enables them to keep their jobs. Some

actors will undertake their roles with a certain flashiness, boldly letting out spontaneous images in a bravura manner, at first, and then beginning the sensitive selection of values and colors as they move toward internalized meanings. Other actors will completely conceal what they are doing, and only when ready, will they permit inner conceptions to surface. In those actors, it is as if the nature of outer detail miraculously grew from the roots of inner detail.

Rehearsals Are Something Special

Rehearsals are adventurous occasions during which you uncover solutions by getting everything to work for you. This is doing one's job in a professional manner. Your immediate concern at the outset of rehearsals, therefore, is to find the means to enable you to perform the role.

When you have previously mapped out the organic ingredients of a role by formulating actions and behavioral choices, you are more prepared to approach rehearsals with streams of imaginative ideas ready to flow. Even though an actor may wish to give full behavior at early rehearsals because of a concern about quickly establishing performance values, it is perhaps best to work by degrees and gradually sense a pattern to follow. However, even working by degrees can create full behavior if one's creative impulses desire such a procedure. Rehearsals are a time for teamwork, with actors working towards a common goal and taking an interest in each other's approach.

Uncertainties will often creep in during rehearsals, but proper preparation will lessen them. In film work, much can go wrong as a scene is prepared and technical disruptions take priority over the actor. Sometimes an actor may feel uneasy when the intensity of a light bulb, or the drape of a curtain may seem to have more importance than the actor. The film actor has to learn how to be comfortable with the rehearsal and preparation time needed by technicians and designers. The long periods of technical interruptions in film work can serve as extra rehearsal time for actors in numerous ways.

Knowing the Director's Territory

It is the director who has the plan of how everything is going to be put together, and the actor should have respect for that kind of effort. Some highly esteemed directors are regarded as parental figures who can magically shape a performance. With such a director, actors can trustingly lend their acting instruments to every detail of the director's vision.

But, many actors know that there are directors who can mar performances by conventional suggestions or by not knowing how to properly help the actor when the actor needs assistance.

Of supreme importance is that you try to help the director by knowing the director's job. Many directors have had acting experience and can have an appreciation for the acting process.

By knowing the director's job, you can easily adjust to varying directorial styles and approaches. Just as you have to find your way into your scenes while preparing alone, you may also discover, particularly in films, that some directors will arrive with incomplete ideas at the beginning of a shooting day and gradually find their way into what is being filmed that day. Directors have been known, both in early rehearsals of a stage play or in the early hours of a film day, to permit actors complete freedom. They will keenly observe the values that actors are ready to bring to a scene and then will skillfully fuse directorial ideas with the actors' contributions. This is perhaps the most satisfyingly creative collaboration between director and actor.

To a large extent, the director deals with imagery. The perceptive actor can contribute to the director's imagery by knowing how to live in an environment. Stage technique can be useful in films because of the constant pictures that a stage actor must paint with the acting instrument while being in a space and moving in it. It may be for this reason that some film directors prefer to work with actors who have had solid stage experience. An actor has not acquired a reliable technique if that technique has not instilled the creative means of self-direction. A solid technique means having a guru within you who is ready to assume a parental role toward you. A director gets a sense of unknown people when studying a script and has to find out about the characters in order to bring them to life through the actors; the actor, likewise, finds out about a character through directorial means. You will work as an actor with two directors; the director within you and the actual director. Both will help you to not only polish your ideas, but will also lead you to do more with a moment.

Pulse and Rhythms

Each of us possesses our own inner pulse and internal rhythm. We feel comfortable with the currents and charges of our rhythms. For this reason, it can be important to find out to what extent you have established a character's rhythm rather than imposing your own pulse and rhythm upon the character.

Going for The Size

There are roles which contain highly charged energy and dynamic transmissions. When there is size in a role, Adler entreats the actor to go with it. She mentions that there are high-level audiences who expect acting with size. This is not what is called acting in a grand manner, but using one's resources to capture the emotional texture of material which has size and scope. Important is the instinctive sense of knowing when to do more and when to do less; when to extend the acting instrument and when to minimize.

An actor must be comfortable with the knowledge that truth comes in different degrees and need not fear a falseness when making sparks fly or riding the big waves of a scene.

Unresolved Matters and Ragged Edges

Knowing what a scene is about is not the same as making the scene happen. A scene happens when the actors have an instinct for finding the problems in a scene and for understanding why it is not happening. The actors also need the instinct for selecting the proper means to solve these problems. This can be either an intuitive process or a conscious preoccupation.

Problems in scenes become present when intentions are blurred or certain colors are lacking, giving a shapeless-ness to scenic values. These are but a few of the numerous problems that can exist in scenes and that need attention. Acting, like any other profession, cannot be accomplished if inherent problems are not solved. You question a scene in the same way that an automobile designer should question his automobile. What are the most and the least successful features? How is the tone of performance being lowered, or even ruptured?

The advice, "Don't create problems where they don't exist" is apt for any actor's work, but when problems are present they are not to be ignored or superficially glossed over. Instead, an attempt should be made to get the deeper richness that problems can offer. Strasberg likened problems to deep layers of diamond deposits. Deep problems can offer a target at which to aim and the more interesting the target, the more interesting will be the solution and expression.

Here are some checkpoints to keep in mind in approaching a scene that you may feel is out of kilter:

...What is your main intention in the scene? Are you accomplishing it in an easy, lazy way and not getting the full logic of character and situation?

...Examine the environment. What problems and obstacles exist in the environment? How can they help you to gain more vivid expression? Problems in an environment are created by both people and physical objects.

...Are you just doing the main trait of a character and playing the obvious? What are the opposites that exist in the character? How can you enrichen them to get intriguing complexities that possess strong realities?

...Are you creating problems that do not exist? A simple straightforward scene may not have problems and all that is necessary is to be aware of the small intentions; if there is a big intention, it will take care of itself.

At the outset of studying a role, you may not be immediately aware of any problems, but may later discover that they do exist and require exploration. As in other creative endeavors, one starts from scratch by discerning the facts through a reexamination of intentions and behavioral choices. In searching for interim solutions, let new ideas happen and permit them to take you where you wish to go without anticipating results.

The tone in which the ideas of the words are being conveyed can cause jarring notes. An actor conveys ideas about the character through the character's words and even when spoken with a sense of dynamics, they can remain monotonous. The dynamics may happen in the way the words are rushed and yet a monotony can be present if the actor believes that a problem has been solved when it really has not been given attention.

Improvisations are often employed to arrive at the essence of a scene. It is important that improvisation not be employed for its own sake by just paraphrasing the words. If an improvisation is used to solve a problem, then one must agitate the imagination to get into deeper layers. New discoveries can occur when you approach an improvisation as if you don't know the scene's situation.

Strasberg often referred to experiments done by scientists when confronted with problems. He pointed out that they have the means for finding solutions and confidence in the techniques of their fields that lead to solutions. Just as the experiment of a scientist can fail, so too can an actor's attempt to grab hold of a role fail; but for both, knowledge can be gained by understanding why what could have worked did not work. A colleague of Thomas Edison asked him why he worked on a certain battery over and over again. "I now know 50,000 ways it won't work" was Edison's reply. Problems, then, require a patient, back-and-forth kind of process.

Being able to solve acting problems, as well as problems in a scene, presages new growth in an actor's work and the end of a phase of learning. A maturing occurs with the realization that problems are not insolvable when approached with technique and variety. Actors seek variety to remedy what they may feel are acting deficiencies. Gielgud mentions that Olivier was much better at this than he, because Olivier was aware of his limitations and acting problems and chose roles to work on them. Olivier, fortunately, was able to use technique to bring off anything he tackled.

Nerves, Blood and Thoughts

Stanislavski made it very clear that when it is time for the actor to act, the actor must act! It is not a time to retreat into a corner and wait for emotion or search for a motivation. He was very specific about this point, arguing that whatever an actor does has to be important to nerves, blood and thoughts. The will required to perform should not force the acting instrument towards expression, as this often results in faking. Forcing the instrument can cause tension, which can stop true expression, and thereby rob the actor's work of the elements that lead to a truly expressive performance.

The essential work in relaxation and sense memory endows the actor with control of the instrument. These skills give the actor means to will the instrument towards a creative state and the ability to continue that willingness once the creative state is underway. Will, as Carl Jung has pointed out, is the only tool a person has and one must take care of it. It is, therefore, the strongest thing the actor needs. The actor can never expect to be fully expressive without will being present. It is needed in order to respond to the content of a scene so that the scene has an immediate aliveness. There are no two ways about it; either the actor comes alive or the actor might as well call it quits and go home.

Confidence has been likened to a two-edged sword because it can make you feel right even when you are wrong. If it leads you to continue to do the wrong things and not re-evaluate your tendencies and beliefs, confidence can be fatal. Conversely, lack of confidence can be beneficial; it is this lack of confidence that can drive a person towards constructive goals. In the history of art, there have been many painters, poets, musicians and other creative people, whose lack of confidence drove them to an overwhelming desire to fulfill themselves as artists. They intuitively knew what was lacking in their artistic pursuits and came to terms with what they would need to both develop and progress. Often, those who are unsure about themselves can get better and surpass those who function with the wrong kind of ego-based confidence. It is important for anyone to acknowledge that obstacles can be conquered and that within everyone there is the capacity to realize the decision to overcome these barriers.

Preliminary Rituals

Every actor is faced with the problem of preparation. It is a means of tuning up the instrument. The actor gradually discovers, during a period of training (or during rehearsals) that less and less time is needed to get ready. With developed skills, preparation can take anywhere from one to five minutes.

A contemporary preparation technique for people in all walks of life is visualization. This involves visualizing a situation in which you might be anxious and seeing yourself performing flawlessly so that the actual experience will be encountered with less anxiety. The goal of visualization is to feel that one is in charge of one's life and has control over an event.

The purpose of preparation is to give you the time needed to stir the emotions and get the adrenalin going. A preparation cannot be a general kind of happening and the more skillful you are, the more knowledgeable you will be about selecting a preparation which is specifically related to the material. Preparation, for that matter, not only takes place off-stage or off-camera, but also during the course of a scene requiring a sudden burst of emotions and thoughts.

Circles of Attention

Concentration is a built-in component of an actor's intentions and behavioral choices. It permits the actor to give attention to the moment being created. What you accomplish by being involved with intentions and choices is to entice an audience (or camera) into participating in the event taking place.

By working with objects and physical activities, exploring the various realities present, you will be able to forget about being watched or filmed. All that matters to you is the object or activities, and more clearly focused moments are the result.

In acting, you are constantly involved with various forms of concentration—mental actions, emotional and physical sensations, physical activities—and it is the quality of your grasp on these elements and your concern with their clarity that enables you to capture attention. You should permit dramatic imagination to soar when giving clarity to points in order to achieve what is often referred to as a performance of interest and color.

Concentration is relaxation since it can not fully occur with tension, strain or awareness of an audience or a film crew. It inspires the actor to use the creative process and has a way of turning nervousness into sensitivity. Concentration is not always easily achieved, and therefore can be lost. Losing one's concentration is normal, but a creative process is still occurring as long as you attempt to get it back.

Bouncing Off the Other Person

The forms of connection between actors vary in style and purpose. Adler recommends that you share an experience with your fellow actors and that you make sure they absorb the ideas you are conveying. Bouncing off the other person for some is not to act, but to react.

Connection between actors is not merely eye contact and listening well, but also perceiving what is going on with the other actor and letting a creative intercourse develop. Actors are at their best when they are influencing one another, sometimes contributing as much as 50% to another's performance. In the best of acting, there is a feeding of each other's reality and a physical freedom with each other.

Clurman said, "An actor who is unable to make contact with another actor is either a self-centered imbecile or no actor at all." Being "no actor at all" implies an inability to make contact with anything in the environment.

There are actors who do not make much eye contact, just as there are non-actors who do not. Researchers, however, have discovered that there are no real conclusions to be made about the psychology of people who do not make contact with others. For character traits, eye contact can be an important touch. Observe closely what internal manifestations are occurring when a person looks away; it may be a manifestation of shyness or part of a person's mental process.

With sensorial and organic impulses in acting, there tends to be less give and take on a verbal level. Nonverbal communication is full and alive when actors are working for dimensional realities, and are therefore more human.

Maneuvering Powers

In some way, the actor needs to remain detached in order to have the proper kind of control and to use the skills of self-observation and self-correction. Numerous times you have to give special attention to what are the big moments in acting. Your control center provides a sense of direction for you and the audience, as you both are being prepared for a big, pivotal moment. You must permit the instrument to go with the moment, abandoning the instrument to the moment and permitting the audience to go with it. This does not imply that you should accomplish the moment with complete abandonment; on the contrary, the element of control is essential, for without it, there lurks the danger of overacting. A violent scene between two actors, for example, has to be approached with a sure degree of control. Some actors have the ability to work an audience up to a high point, only to abandon the audience and permit it to ride the crest. This can be an impressive ingredient in the actor's ability to maneuver powers of the acting instrument.

Don't Saw the Air with Your Arms and Hands

The problem of what to do with the arms and hands has plagued numerous performers. Actors, like anyone else, can tend to be illustrative in their gestures in order to emphasize what is being said. This is at the heart of what is termed verbal use of the arms and hands. Showy gestures can result from not being able to control the surplus energy of the acting instrument. Energy, however, which is a vital part of acting, can be used to create new and interesting expressions with sensorial and visceral body experiences.

Strasberg was very insistent on quelling verbal movements of the arms and hands, because, after long years of keen observation, he concluded that they kill and censor rich impulses that can be put to better use.

A strong image to keep in mind is that the arms and hands have a vocabulary of their own and need not be caught up in verbal rhythms and patterns. Adler suggests that you reach out with ideas and not your hands.

Lows and Highs on the Dial

Certain actors have the unique gift of being able to perform any emotion or style; they can do anything.

Spontaneous and powerfully free-flowing emotions can be witnessed in many human events. Television permits us to observe human beings in moments of elation, sorrow, anger—the entire emotional spectrum. Human beings in very human situations burn our TV screens: athletes at a Rose Bowl football game create a wide range of emotions of concern, weeping, joy, anger, resignation and triumphal ecstasy. One cannot help but be impressed by how these types of TV events capture drama in a humanly convincing way.

Any actor, consciously or unconsciously, continually tunes into emotions in the day-to-day environment. Some actors will live in certain areas when preparing for a role in order to capture the emotional tone of the locale through the clues and suggestions that can be gleaned from the environment.

As human beings, actors have the potential for experiencing every human feeling, thought and sensation, but their task is not just a matter of creating real emotion; they must give it artistic form. This involves the ability to gauge the level on which to act the emotion. A bombastic, eruptive emotion in life can have its particular force, but that kind of force in acting can be operatic overacting.

Going With Your Impulses

Physiologically, impulses are part of the human nervous system's functioning, with the brain acting as a central switchboard, automatically sending and receiving messages to and from the nervous system. Impulse has to do with opening and closing the "gates" in your body which create controlled nuances. These are the nuances which engage an audience.

Sensorial technique exercises create channels through which impulses can become expressive, thus giving Method acting training its value and popularity. Impulses and responses that function on a low expressive level indicate an inability to maneuver impulses into expressive channels. An actor in touch with moving impulses not only experiences transforming energies, but, most of all, is able to transport the audience to other levels of consciousness.

APPENDIX

Relaxation Exercise

The relaxation field already exists in you. The exercise is a time of self-affirmation, a time to love yourself and a time to know your uniqueness. Have an amiable encounter with yourself and tell yourself that your talent is unique. Give yourself this feedback at regular intervals throughout the exercise.

In a standing position, sense a draining of energy in all your physical and mental areas. Physical areas are the neck, shoulders, torso, arms, hands, pelvic area, legs and feet. Mental areas are the temples, brow, bridge of the nose, eyelids, eyeballs, optic nerves, the temple-nerves at the side of the eyes, scalp, cheeks, jaw and mouth.

Be aware of visually seizing on any objects around you. Avoid any sharp focusing. The eyes should not blink or flutter during the entire exercise. The lids are very active and alert during our daily activities. If the eyes tend to blink at any time during the exercise, it is best to gently close the lids because blinking can only perpetuate more blinking. By closing the lids, you can perhaps deal more effectively with the eyeballs and optic nerves, which may be causing some of the blinking. Blinking can also be caused by thinking about the exercise.

The jaw should always be loose and hanging from its hinges. The temporal-mandibular joint is the area where the jaw joins the skull. It enables the lower jaw to be extremely flexible in movement. Move the jaw around at intervals. Move it gently to the left and right; create easy circles. The flexibility of the jaw can be related to the pelvis; strong emotions often abide in both areas.

Energizing is also a popular form of relaxation. Energizing is accomplished by tensing each area of the body and then relaxing, starting with the feet and working upwards to areas of the head.

You can alternate draining of energy with energizing by first energizing and then proceeding to the oozing out of physical and mental energies.

HANGING LOOSE

Loosening, as with breathing, is the most accessible means of relaxing the body and mind. Some people prefer it under certain circumstances when they lack the time to abide by a systematically prescribed procedure.

You loosen by voluntarily shaking off stress, kinks, knots, and tight muscles. Empty yourself of any physical discomfort.

Make expressive dance movements to release tense muscles. Shake like a leaf, stretch or do push-ups. Go through an aerobic dance routine.

Zero in on the neck, the area of common stress. Let your head go back; roll it around and do neck circles 10 to 15 times.

Squeeze the eyes and then relax them. Move the jaw left and right, up and down. Alternately energize (make faces) and relax the facial muscles.

Melt like butter and feel your arms hang like spaghetti. Relax the many strings of nerves that cling to muscles.

Feel your head, eyes, lids, jaw, brain and neck become like one big marshmallow.

Sense pent-up energy in the body draining through imaginary valves at the tips of the fingers and toes. Let the fingers drip loosely from the knuckles.

What areas of tightness have you discovered? Loosen the tight areas by moving them. When you feel a tense area relaxing, get a feeling of the relaxation spreading through the body.

Let out explosive sounds as you move hinges and sockets in the arms, shoulders, hips and legs.

Breathe and direct oxygen through the bronchial tubes as you expand the lungs. Empty the lungs abruptly.

Direct oxygen into your diaphragm—the partition between chest and abdomen. Expel air with your diaphragm muscles as you blow it out of the mouth.

SITTING DOWN

Gradually lower yourself into a chair, maintaining the relaxation of mental areas. Melt into the chair as you slump down with legs spread out in a comfortable position, heels resting on the floor. Try not to be concerned about sitting on the edge of the chair and being about to slip off. Let the arms hang loose. Go into a corpse position. Shut out all external sounds. Return and listen to the sounds of your body—arterial sounds, pulsations, stomach gurgles, heartbeat, head noises and breathing.

Try not to assume the same position in the chair each time you do the exercise. A position that is relaxing on one occasion may not be the most relaxing for another. Move around in the chair until you find a comfortable position. Sometimes having the right or left leg stretched out can be more comfortable than stretching both legs. When making adjustments, use only the muscles in the area you are adjusting, e.g., if you wish to move the legs into a more comfortable position, keep the rest of the body relaxed and motionless. You do not need to tighten the jaw muscles or let the upper body go forward in order to adjust the muscles of the legs; this principle also applies to adjusting the arms or other body parts.

Avoid holding onto the sides of the chair and let the arms dangle loosely or have one or both hands rest on your thighs.

If you find an area which is tense, simply give yourself a pleasant command to relax that area. Avoid shaking out tension by moving your arms, legs or neck. Permit the wonderful capacity of the brain to relax tense areas. During performance, if you feel tension creeping into the shoulders or legs, you cannot stop a scene and shake out the tension. But by training the capacity of the mind to send messages to tense areas, you develop the ability to relax while performing. There are always moments in a scene when you can check for tensions. In sending a message to different areas of the body and hidden places, feel the message travel soothingly along the nerve circuitry.

As you slump down in the chair, feel the floor upon which all the weight of the legs bears down—as if your legs and feet are on a scale. Permit the chair to absorb all of your weight, tensions and muscular feelings.

If your fingers tend to wiggle and move (a common happening in daily life) discover the nerve routes up the arms, across the shoulders, including the back of the neck. The fingers (and toes) are connected to nerve routes and that is why both hands and feet can simultaneously have excessive little movements. Relax the nerve routes and the wiggling movements will diminish considerably.

Tension in a forefinger is not tension in a small and insignificant area, but can easily involve a whole group of muscles. Tension in the right forefinger, for example, may have begun somewhere on the left side of the body and travelled over a whole group of muscles before manifesting itself in the right forefinger.

Keep the fingers limp and not turned inwards. Fingers which are turned inwards may be caused by the way your cartilage is formed, but it is for you to discover whether this is so or not. Tension in the hands, particularly the fingers, is frequently overlooked.

The head need not be in a straight upward position, but can droop forward with the chin resting on the chest; or the head can hang to one side or the other.

Pause a while as you explore outer and inner areas during your physical relaxation and let the head go back gently. When you let the head hang back, it may at first be uncomfortable, but in time you will discover it can hang back for any length of time. Be sure that you keep the mental areas relaxed as the head goes back and returns to a forward position. The forward position can be one in which the head alternately hangs to the sides. If you feel the mental areas become more relaxed as the head moves forward, it may mean that there has been some holding on in the neck.

If there is any problem in getting a general mental relaxation while working specifically on the physical, you can alternate the two. For example, specifically relax the legs, but before moving to another physical area, check the relaxation of the mental areas. The ultimate aim of the exercise, however, is to simultaneously relax both areas on a moment's notice—an ever-present demand from audition to performance.

BREATHING

Following are a number of choices for breathing and you may wish to try them all.

Just sitting and breathing can be totally relaxing; it can be done for a few minutes or as long as 15 minutes.

Feel the oxygen enter your nose, moving into the nostrils and passing through the nose hairs as it subsequently moves down into parts of the body. Holistic practitioners advise you to breathe deeply through the nose and feel it go to your center which is slightly below the navel.

Establish an even rhythm as you breathe in relaxation. Let your mind and body go with the exhalation as you breathe out tensions and harmful carbon dioxides.

Establish a breathing rhythm by inhaling on a count of six, hold for a count of three and exhale on a count of six. The count can change from one occasion to another, and you may wish to formulate the count to suit the moment. Repeat the cycle as often as you wish.

Are you exhaling interfering or unwanted thoughts? Give in to their expiration. Breathe deep into the body, all the way down to the balls of the feet. Some Yogis breathe slowly through the mouth and exhale slowly through the nose.

Are there constrictions in the neck area adjoining the top of the spine? Are there constrictions in such areas as the stomach or pelvis? Breathe into and exhale from those areas. Visualize the life-giving force of oxygen going into all the organs of the body. Some suggest letting the air go out through the buttocks instead of the nostrils.

You can direct oxygen to areas of pain and discomfort. Permit the oxygen to purify such areas and then exhale the impurities and contaminants through a relaxed jaw and mouth. Not all oxygen goes to the lungs; 35% of it goes to the brain and you can direct inhalation to cleanse affected areas. Direct the oxygen to a pain and imagine the exhalation actually going through the flesh and skin covering the pain area.

Esoteric breathing images have been beneficial for many people. Breathe the sun into the whole body and breathe out moon energy. Surround yourself with golden light and breathe it in.

TESTING MENTAL AREAS

Let all mental areas melt: the temples, brow, bridge of nose, eyelids, eyeballs, optic nerves, the temple-nerves at the side of the eyes; loosen the scalp; feel energy dripping out of the cheeks; let the jaw hang loosely with teeth and lips comfortably separated. Relax the jaw hinges through which pass most of the nerve circuits from the brain which send messages to the body. Loosen any holding on in the jaw hinges.

Relax the face so that deep interior qualities can surface and be seen in relaxed facial muscles. Long-distance runners have discovered that they waste calories by tightening the muscles of the face. By relaxing the face, they put the calories to use to help them run faster. During a peak emotion in acting, a relaxed face will permit the dynamics of an inner emotion to create more interesting facial nuances.

Refrain from blinking. Let the eyelids open slightly and heavily. Close the partially open lids as if they are weights sinking slowly into water. Repeat this a few times. Let the lids come together gently. The partial, sleepy-like opening and closing of the lids should be done at several intervals during the physical relaxation.

As you maintain the relaxation of the mental areas, gently let the head go back. As the head goes back, feel the tiny vertebrae in the neck. Let the head hang back for a while as you sense a general releasing of the nerves throughout the body beginning from the ganglia of nerves in the back of the neck.

Bring the head forward and let it droop to the side or hang forward. Do neck circles.

DEEPER PHYSICAL RELAXATION

Although many disciplines attempt to shut out any distracting sound, some people are unable to accomplish this in all circumstances. In that event, find a way of using sound as a focus. A student in my workshop had great difficulty with mental relaxation at the beginning of the relaxation period. After many months, he heard a cat meowing in an adjoining church garden, and by going with the sound, he was able to relax more quickly. I suggested that he choose a sensory stimulus at the beginning of his relaxation by creating an inner sanctuary of sounds and smells of the sea, a meadow, a forest or other locales. He was to continue this process until he felt he could mentally relax more quickly, knowing that he could always return to sensory stimuli when difficulties reoccurred. Since the performer works under many types of trying circumstances, this example demonstrates that you can always find a solution in the balance between yourself and your professional surroundings.

In your sitting position, feel the stretching taking place in your body. Relax the large muscle groups in the arms and legs, including the hands and feet. Sequentially, begin to relax other areas, particularly the hidden areas in the armpits, back of the neck and the small of the back. Investigate the pelvic area in which there can be a lot of holding on, particularly in the genitalia and anus areas.

Now you are ready to journey into the body as your conscious thoughts pass through and monitor the recesses of tissues, muscles, flesh, fibers, tendons, etc. You are now permitting your body and mind to collaborate. Although you will be sending forth commands from the mind to relax discovered body tensions, try not to regard those commands as strict and authoritative, but part of pleasant discoveries.

The journey into the body should be a fresh experience each time you do the exercise. Rid yourself of muscular battles and calmly be your own monitor as you get into the organs, flesh and muscles which surround the bones. Sense the flesh and the beautiful latticework within it. Some people relax right down to their bones.

FINDING YOUR CENTER

When you are physically relaxed, you are ready to begin the mental relaxation. During the physical part of the exercise, you partially relaxed mental areas and now are prepared to work on them more specifically.

Give yourself a final check while still slumped down in the chair. Are you still physically relaxed in all areas? Tension moves around and a tension you may have eliminated in one area may have moved into another area.

Gradually draw the legs towards you until the feet are comfortably apart (about 10 or 12 inches) and pointing forward. Let the legs design a right angle position with a straight line going out from the hips to the knees and another straight line from the knees down through the ankles. The space between the knees and ankles should be equal and the thighs and calves in a parallel position. The toes and knees should point directly ahead. Sense an energy proceeding in a forward direction from all these areas.

As you move from the physical position into an aligned position for the mental, you may find it helpful to first visualize your body in alignment before executing the necessary movements. Visualize a comfortable alignment, rather than any kind of position that requires effort.

Without thrusting the upper part of the body forward (including the head/neck area), gently move into a sitting position, pressing lightly against the floor with the balls of your feet to give you a little leverage. At the same time begin to align the head, neck and spine. When you have completed the movement, the upper and lower body should be aligned. Keep the jaw relaxed and eyelids heavy as you do the movement. After the movement is completed, check for relaxation in the buttocks, small of the back and leg muscles—all of which were used to make the movement.

You should not think of the aligned position as rigid or overly postural, but one that is comfortable and centered. Feel energy traveling up and down the spine and from the small neck vertabrae into the head.

Permit the head to sit easily on the neck without any leaning forward, backward or to the sides. Make adjustments by contacting the swivel bone in the neck. Often a proper alignment of the head and neck can be accomplished by having a sense of moving only the top of the head to the left or right until it is centered. Effective alignment can also be attained by moving only the chin to the left or right. Observe these adjustments in a mirror.

Finding your center is an artistic responsibility; it is creating your own circle. In this exercise, you are only asked to keep the body aligned for a short period of time. Yogis and Swamis do it for up to nine hours.

The alignment position may seem uncomfortable in the beginning, but will not remain so. It is optional whether or not your back touches the back of the chair. In Zen meditation, sitting in a chair is the easiest of five meditation positions. It is based on the ancient Egyptian method of meditational sitting. You may eventually have the feeling that you are not sitting on a chair at all, but that your body is floating. Permit the chair to accept the weight of your body as you maintain a comfortable alignment. Find your own center in the way you would find the center (or off-center) of a character—a prim character will have a tight center, while a lopsided type will have an asymmetrical center. Notice the comfortable center of some notable people during interview talk shows on television.

Feel an energy flow in your alignment—from the base of the spine up to the head and back down the spine again. Maintaining alignment is greatly helped if you think of the neck as a bridge between the body and the head, rather than letting it be an improper barrier. Even people who have had a broken back, or have a spinal problem, are able to find ways of giving a semblance of alignment.

When you are in an aligned position, sense how the inner organs are not pressing against one another as they may have been in the slumped down physical position. Contact the smooth flow not only in the organs but throughout the body.

Learn how to introduce a more harmonious center to your daily activities. Sometimes, balance and peace can be rare in our private lives. We know we have the capacity to attain it, but often lack the patience and neglect to take the necessary time.

DEEPER MENTAL RELAXATION

Mental relaxation is more important than physical relaxation, but for many it is not easily attainable. Physical tension is more observable than mental tension. Mental tension is observable in a tense face, wrinkled brow or tight lips. However, even without these facial mannerisms, mental tension can still function almost invisibly, deep within mental areas.

Begin to be aware of any thoughts and permit them to float away. Become detached from them. You cannot always stop your thoughts, even with effort, but you can let them disappear into the space around you. Try not to be an audience for your thoughts. Let them find an audience elsewhere. When you control the thinking process and mentally relax, you are relaxing the left brain where more chattering goes on than in the right brain.

These are the areas to further relax: the temples, the brow (including the scalp and the bridge of the nose) the entire eye area (lids, eyeballs and optic nerves) and areas of the cheeks, mouth and jaw. Particular emphasis is placed on the jaw as tension here may mirror a deeper tension elsewhere in the body's organs and muscles. Some people feel less stomach discomfort when they learn how to relax a tight jaw.

The first mental area relates to the overloaded circuitry of the temples, with its network of blue nerves and blood vessels which feed into the brain. The temples are not just at the side of the head but extend to the side of the eyes. The temple nerves actually enter into the eyelids. Visualize the temples as being in knots and unravel them; let them be as loose as jelly as you control the flow of blood in the temple areas. Preferably, keep the lids gently closed until it is time to work with the eye area.

Glide into the forehead area. Let the brow and bridge of the nose melt. As the forehead melts, sense the entire scalp loosening. The forehead muscles are important since they are directly related to the relaxation of scalp, neck and upper part of the body. Check for any tension across the top of the eyebrows. Feel a gentle flow between the skin layers of the scalp and the skull. Sense the flow all the way to the back of the head. Sometimes there can be a low awareness of the tightness that exists at the back of the head. As with all mental areas, feel a calm radiating all over the scalp area.

Mental relaxation is not only free self-analysis but also a free facial treatment as wrinkles and lines caused by tension begin to dissolve.

Gradually move into the areas of the eyes. First melt the muscles around the eyes. Let the lids be gently together or have a very slight opening so that only a slit of light enters. Relax the optic nerve tracts that meet inside the back of the head and then move into the brain's two hemispheres. This is why the optic nerves and brain are really the same organ. The optic nerves are actually extensions of the brain.

Eighty percent of the information we receive is through the eyes, which accounts for the eye area being a source of tension. Not only are the eyes the chief source of information, but they also report our state of mind. They use up a lot of energy during daily activities and our whole being is affected when that energy creates a tense state.

Let the energy in the eyelids melt and ooze down the side of the nose onto the cheeks. Make sure that both the eyeballs and eyelids are relaxed. Sometimes the eyelids may be relaxed but the eyeballs are not, or vice versa.

Begin to open the lids with one-quarter or one-third openings. Sense their heaviness as you open them slightly and feel them sinking when you close them. It is advisable to start with small openings. The muscles which open and close the lids may need to be retrained in order to get smooth, heavy, uninterrupted openings and closings. This retraining is often necessary to prepare you for half-way openings and closings. The final goal in this process is, of course, full opening and closing with heavy, relaxed lids.

The movement of the lids should be an uninterrupted gliding movement with no staircase stops and flutterings. When the lids close, feel them sink like a weight in water as they skim lightly downward over the eyeballs. When you open the eyes all the way, be aware of any tendency to blink rapidly. If sudden blinking occurs, gently hold the lids open, contact the blinking muscles and get them under control and then let the lids sink heavily. There may be burning in the eyes when you first work with them, even tears, but that will disappear with time and patience. If you wear contact lenses, you can train the lids so the lenses need not be an interference.

Sense the eyeballs float in the vitreous fluid that surrounds them.

In a workshop setting, look at the environment in a relaxing way without any blinking at lights, moving objects or people. Take only a nominal interest in them. You may even want to softly focus on an object and shut out all others. Calmly blink as you focus on the object in order to avoid staring at it.

Feel the relaxation of the eyelids, eyeballs and the brow move gently into the head area—from the front of the brain to the back of the brain.

The heaviness in half-open eyelids is one that occurs in a meditator's alpha state, or in biofeedback. The alpha state, as you know, permits deep creative intuitions to surface.

Relaxation of the eyes cannot be overemphasized for the film actor, as many film nuances occur with the eyes. The more the film actor is able to relax the eyes, the greater will be the range of nuances.

The next area, the cheeks, has more muscles than any part of the face. This is why emotion often registers strongly in the cheeks. The cheeks also indicate our state of health, just as the eyes can reveal our state of mind. Let the muscles and nerve endings of the cheeks melt away.

A Beverly Hills beauty salon has experimented with biofeedback instruments to relax areas of the face in order to prevent wrinkles that result from tense facial mannerisms. The art of relaxing the tiny facial muscles is your own natural biofeedback and far less costly than salon treatments. Constant tension in the forehead or muscles around the mouth can cause permanent lines and wrinkles. This may also give you some insight as to how our inner organs are marked during prolonged states of stress.

The jaw and mouth are the final areas. In life we are always ready to form words and the speech mechanisms are always active, even in a nonverbal state. The mouth itself is a very active area not only for speech but also for the fulfillment of other daily needs, mostly pleasurable. The tongue is an exceptionally strong muscle and should be relaxed just as any other body muscle. Feel all the energy drain from the mouth, lips, tongue and jaw. Having the jaw relaxed does not mean you have to be a mouth breather during the exercise nor should you be concerned if you look somewhat asthmatic.

The strength of the jaw is known by anthropologists who have discovered several human jaw fossils that date back as much as five million years. It is conclusive proof that it is our strongest skeletal area. In three notable anthropological findings since 1974, the remainder of the bodies belonging to jaw fossils had become dust. We might say that the relaxation exercise concludes with attention to one of our strongest and most enduring areas.

Relaxation, Strasberg constantly said, is worked on in the same manner as a Jesuit works daily for a deepening faith in God. As with meditation, it is a purifying experience enabling transformations. Both meditation and relaxation teach one how to tap hidden energies. When there has been complete faith in developing powers of relaxation, you discover that only a few minutes are needed to reach a state where you are receiving the creative blessings of hidden energies.

Action Choices

TO ADMIRE THE WORLD
TO ADMIT PAST MISTAKES
TO ADVISE
TO ANNIHILATE THE TYRANTS
TO ARGUE THE POINT
TO ARRIVE AT THE LAST STOP
TO ASSAULT
TO ASSERT MYSELF
TO ATTACK
TO AVOID
TO AVOID BEING TRACKED DOWN
TO AVOID DELICATE MATTERS
TO AVOID DOING THE INEVITABLE
TO AVOID THE ISSUE
TO AVOID THE TRUTH
TO AWAKEN

TO BAIT
TO BE CONNECTED
TO BE IN HARMONY
TO BE ON GUARD AGAINST
TO BEAT DOWN
TO BLAST
TO BLUFF MY WAY
TO BOLSTER UP
TO BOMB THEM WITH MY POWER
TO BREAK LOOSE
TO BREAK OUT OF MY SHELL
TO BREAK THE BALANCE
TO BRING OUT THE CORRUPT NATURE
TO BRING THEM TO THEIR KNEES
TO BRUISE
TO BRUSH OVER DELICATE MATTERS
TO BURN ALL MY BRIDGES
TO BURST FORWARD

TO CALL THE NEXT MOVE
TO CAPTIVATE
TO CAPTIVATE PEOPLE
TO CAPTIVATE THEIR IMAGINATION
TO CAPTURE
TO CARRY OUT AN IMPORTANT MISSION
TO CAST OFF MEDIOCRITY
TO CAST OFF THE YOKE
TO CAST OUT THE DEVIL
TO CATCH THE EYE
TO CHANGE THE MOOD
TO CHANGE THEIR MINDS
TO CHEW UP AND SPIT OUT
TO CLAIM MY POSITION
TO CLIMB OUT OF MYSELF
TO CLING
TO COOL THINGS OFF
TO COME OUT ON TOP

TO COMPLAIN
TO COMPLETE AN IMPORTANT MISSION
TO CON EVERYONE
TO CONFUSE EVERYTHING
TO CONNECT TO MY DREAM
TO CONNECT WITH THE WORLD
TO CONTAIN MY MOMENTS
TO CONTROL PEOPLE
TO COVER UP MY GUILT
TO CUT THE CRAP
TO CUT THROUGH THE FOG

TO DEFEND WHAT IS MINE
TO DELVE INTO MY FANTASIES
TO DEMAND RECOGNITION
TO DEMAND THEIR BEST
TO DERAIL
TO DESTROY
TO DEVASTATE MY SURROUNDINGS
TO DICTATE THE LAW
TO DISCOVER THE HUMOR OF IT
TO DISCOVER THE TRUTH
TO DO MY WORK
TO DO THE INEVITABLE
TO DO WHAT I HAVE TO DO
TO DO WHATEVER I PLEASE
TO DOMINATE EVERYTHING
TO DRAW THE LINE

TO ENCOURAGE EVERYONE
    TO LOVE THE WORLD
TO ENFORCE MY WILL
TO ENLIGHTEN
TO ESCAPE INTO ANOTHER WORLD
TO EVADE THE ISSUE
TO EXAMINE MY FOLLY
TO EXCITE SOMEONE

TO EXPLAIN WHERE I'M COMING FROM
TO EXPLORE IN DETAIL
TO EXPOSE
TO EXPOSE THE S.O.B.

TO FACE UP TO
TO FIGHT BACK
TO FIGHT FOR WHAT I BELIEVE IN
TO FIGHT THE LIE
TO FIGURE OUT
TO FIND A PLACE FOR MYSELF
TO FIND MY BEARINGS
TO FIND OUT
TO FIND PROTECTION
TO FIND SOMETHING TO DO
TO FIND THE ANSWER
TO FIND THE DIVIDING LINE
TO FIND THE TRUTH
TO FLOW FROM ROOTS TO FLOWERS
TO FLOW WITH THE TIDE
TO FLUSH THEM OUT
TO FLY INTO THE WIND
TO FLY THE COOP
TO FOLLOW
TO FOLLOW MY STAR
TO FORCE CONNECTION
TO FORM A BOND WITH THOSE ABOUT ME
TO FREE MYSELF
TO FREEZE THE BLOOD

TO GET ALL I CAN
TO GET ALONG
TO GET AWAY FROM PEOPLE
TO GET BACK ON COURSE
TO GET BACK TO A BETTER TIME
TO GET IN BED
TO GET IN EVERYWHERE
TO GET IT ALL OUT

TO GET NEXT TO
TO GET OFF THE HOT SEAT
TO GET ON THE GOOD SIDE
TO GET OUT OF MYSELF
TO GET RID OF SOMEONE
TO GET THE UPPER HAND
TO GET THEIR ATTENTION
TO GET THEM OFF MY BACK
TO GET THINGS IN FOCUS
TO GET TO THE POINT
TO GET UNDER THEIR SKIN
TO GIVE MYSELF
TO GO ALL THE WAY
TO GO BACK IN TIME
TO GO FOR IT
TO GO OFF INTO MY OWN WORLD
TO GO ONE STEP FURTHER
TO GO WHERE NO MAN HAS GONE BEFORE
TO GO WITH THE FLOW
TO GROPE IN THE DARK
TO GROSS THEM OUT
TO GUIDE

TO HAUL OVER THE COALS
TO HEAL
TO HEAR THE RESULTS
TO HIT THE BULL'S EYE
TO HOLD FAST TO TRADITION
TO HOLD MYSELF TOGETHER
TO HOLD ONTO SOMEONE
TO HOLD ONTO MY BEARINGS
TO HOLD THEIR INTEREST
TO HOLD UP

TO INCITE
TO INCLUDE ANOTHER
TO INDUCE
TO INFLAME

TO INFLAME YOUR BRAIN
TO INSTIGATE
TO INTIMIDATE
TO INVESTIGATE
TO INVITE
TO INVOLVE THEM IN MY EXPERIENCE

TO JOKE WITH THEM
TO JUMP AT THE CHANCE
TO JUMP IN

TO KEEP A SAFE DISTANCE
TO KEEP AN OPEN MIND
TO KEEP EVERYTHING
TO KEEP FROM RIPPING OUT THEIR GUTS
TO KEEP FROM BEING DESTROYED
TO KEEP FROM SINKING
TO KEEP GOING
TO KEEP IN TOUCH WITH PEOPLE
TO KEEP MYSELF ATTACHED TO PEOPLE
TO KEEP THE LID ON
TO KEEP THE SITUATION IN HAND
TO KEEP THINGS GOING MY WAY
TO KEEP THINGS MY WAY
TO KNOW WHEN ENOUGH IS ENOUGH

TO LEAD BY THE NOSE
TO LEAD INTO A TRAP
TO LEAP THE BULL
TO LEARN HOW TO CONNECT
TO LEND MYSELF TO THE SITUATION
TO LET IT OUT
TO LEVEL
TO LIBERATE THE OPPRESSED
TO LISTEN
TO LIVE IT UP
TO LIVE MOMENT-TO-MOMENT
TO LOOK ON THE BRIGHT SIDE OF LIFE

TO LOOK OUT FOR NUMBER ONE
TO LUNGE FORWARD

TO MAINTAIN MY BALANCE
TO MAKE BOLD MY POINT OF VIEW
TO MAKE A PLACE FOR MYSELF
TO MAKE A SIMPLE CONNECTION
TO MAKE A SLEAZY DEAL
TO MAKE A STAND
TO MAKE THEM ACKNOWLEDGE MY PRESENCE
TO MAKE THEM HUNGER FOR MORE
TO MAKE THEM UNDERSTAND
TO MAKE THINGS COMFORTABLE
TO MAP UNCHARTED TERRITORY
TO MEET MY GOD'S VENGEANCE
TO MOCK EVERYONE
TO MOLD
TO MOVE FROM THE CENTER

TO NAIL
TO NURTURE THOSE AROUND ME

TO OBSERVE EVERYTHING
TO OWN THIS PLACE

TO PAY THEM BACK
TO PESTER
TO PICK UP THE PIECES
TO PIERCE THE UNIVERSE
TO PLANT A SEED OF DOUBT
TO PLEAD MY CASE
TO PLEASE
TO POSSESS EVERYTHING
TO PRACTICE LIKE A CHILD
TO PREPARE MYSELF FOR LOVE
TO PREPARE TO POUNCE
TO PREVAIL
TO PROBE
TO PROTECT A FRIEND

TO PROTECT MYSELF
TO PROVOKE
TO PRY SOME CONFIDENTIAL INFORMATION
TO PULL THE STRINGS
TO PURSUE AN ATTRACTION
TO PUSH MY CASE
TO PUSH THEIR BUTTONS
TO PUT A JEWEL IN YOUR CROWN
TO PUT THEM ON THE SPOT
TO PUT ON ICE
TO PUT THE WORLD IN ORDER
TO PUT TO PROOF

TO QUESTION EVERYTHING
TO QUIET

TO RAM IT HOME UNFLINCHINGLY
TO REACH MY CENTER
TO REALIZE A DREAM
TO REBEL AGAINST
TO REFUSE

TO REGAIN MY CONFIDENCE
TO REMIND
TO REMOVE MYSELF FROM THE SITUATION
TO RESIST
TO RESPOND
TO RESPOND TO THE CALL OF LIFE
TO RETAIN A SENSE OF MYSELF
TO RIP SOMEBODY'S GUTS OUT
TO ROUSE
TO RULE WITH POWER
TO RULE THE ROOST

TO SAVE MYSELF
TO SAVE THE WORLD
TO SCAR
TO SEDUCE
TO SEE ALL VIEWPOINTS

TO SEE IT THROUGH TO THE END
TO SEE NO WHERE TO GO
TO SEE THE HORROR
TO SEE THE WORLD THROUGH A CHILD'S EYES
TO SEE THROUGH THE FOG
TO SEEK COMFORT
TO SEEK GREENER PASTURES
TO SEEK HIDDEN TREASURE
TO SEEK ROMANCE
TO SEIZE AN OPPORTUNITY
TO SELL A BILL OF GOODS
TO SET ON FIRE
TO SETTLE IN A DREAM
TO SHAPE
TO SHARE MY SPACE
TO SHOW WHO'S THE BOSS
TO SHUT OUT THE WORLD
TO SHUT OUT THE NIGHTMARE
TO SMASH
TO SNEAK THROUGH THE BACK DOOR
TO SOAK UP EVERYTHING
TO SOLVE A PROBLEM
TO SPIN MY WEB
TO SPIRITUALLY LEAD
TO SPOIL THE PARTY
TO SPRING THE TRAP
TO SQUIRM THROUGH
TO STAB
TO STAND MY GROUND
TO STATE MY INTENTIONS
TO STIR
TO STOP THIS
TO STRAIGHTEN THEM OUT
TO SWIM AGAINST

TO TAKE A CHANCE
TO TAKE CARE OF
TO TAKE CHARGE OF TODAY
TO TAKE IN HAND
TO TANTALIZE
TO TEAR BACK TO THE RAW ELEMENTS
TO TELL IT LIKE IT IS
TO TELL THE WHOLE TRUTH
TO THINK BIG
TO THROW OFF THE RAILS
TO TOWER OVER
TO TRAP MY PREY
TO TRY TO DO SOMETHING
TO TRY TO FIND AN ANSWER
TO TRY TO HIT THE TARGET

TO UNDERMINE

TO URGE

TO WAIT IT OUT
TO WEAKEN THE DEFENSES
TO WIN AT ANY COST
TO WIN SOMEONE OVER

Section Examples for Scene Work and Monologues

The following are examples of scene work and monologues done by students in my workshop.

GIVEN CIRCUMSTANCE
To carry out an important mission
Overall chill
Place - visual
Personal object
SECTIONS
1. *To keep in touch with people*
   Overall sun
   Place - visual and smell
2. *To stab*
   Pain - migraine headache
   Stimuli - butterflies in the stomach
3. *To escape into another world*
   Place - visual
   Personal object
   Overall steam
   Wandering personal object
4. *To resist*
   Sound - irritating
   Taste - ecky horrible
5. *To keep things my way*
   Place - visual and sound

GIVEN CIRCUMSTANCE
To keep it in my family
Smell of ozone
SECTIONS
1. *To hide my feelings*
   Vocal characterization - bumble bee in throat
   Vocal characterization - anchor pulling down in chest
2. *To bait*
   Personal object - knife
   Cold shower down spine and legs
3. *To ease my guilt*
   Towel flick behind knees
   Goldenseal herb in mouth
4. *To face my separate destiny*
   Sound of a song
   Place - strawberry spring
5. *To seek help*
   Place - barn
6. *To keep a distance*
   Wandering personal object of Aunt's nose
7. *To disarm*
   Sound of Dhyani organ music
   Personal object - a lamb
8. *To trap*
   Extreme overall cold

GIVEN CIRCUMSTANCE
To inspect my surroundings
Place (sight, sound and aromas of Times Square)
SECTIONS
1. *To bolster up and spill it out*
   Extreme overall cold (ice and wind)
   Alcohol rush from stomach and throat to head
2. *To explore the world of my fantasies*
   Sharp smell of mint from lips to the nose
   Alcohol rush from head to feet
3. *To greet the fear of death*
   Overall sunshine
   Extreme sauna heat on the face
4. *To seek shelter*
   Wind rush on head
   Overall extreme cold (ice)
5. *To seek his love*
   Overall sunshine
   Jack hammer in legs
6. *To practice as a child*
   Song in eyes, lips, jaw, throat and chest
7. *To fight back*
   Sound of a record scratch
   Sharp smell of exhaust
   Sharp taste of cigarettes
   Sound of jack hammer in legs
8. *To let it out*
   Song in lips, eyes and throat
   Overall sunshine
   Extreme sauna heat on face

GIVEN CIRCUMSTANCE
To open up and tell the truth
Heat on face
Stimuli - dizziness
SECTIONS
1. *To seize an opportunity*
   Wandering personal object - a brush
   Vocal characterization - inability to swallow
2. *To force a connection*
   Place - visual of a ship
   Overall humid air
3. *To find myself*
   Wandering personal object - fur piece
   Overall warm wind
   Headache
4. *To make my point*
   Wandering object - feather
   Overall sunshine
   Smell of vodka
5. *To understand*
   Fast wandering objects - ice cubes
   Overall slightly cold wind
   Stimuli - rapid heart beat
6. *To back up*
   Stimuli - rapid heart beat
   Overall very hot sun
7. *To explain*
   Overall fog
8. *To make my point*
   Pain in stomach
   Wandering personal object - blanket piece
   Smell of rubbing alcohol

THE TRANSPERSONAL ACTOR
Reinterpreting Stanislavski
by Ned Manderino

The Transpersonal Actor is an internationally accepted technique book and a valuable supplement to the Stanislavski principles contained in *All About Method Acting*. The book clearly presents innovative technique theory and exercises that re-emphasize Stanislavski's desire to see further development of his System.

What they've said about *The Transpersonal Actor*

"One of the most refreshing and practical books on acting to emerge since the works of Boleslavsky and Stanislavski. An inspired collection of images, exercises and other helpful aids."
Stacy Keach

"An excellent textbook. Stanislavski would have been proud."
JoAnne Meredith
Former Executive Director
Lee Strasberg Institute

"The most thorough adaptation of Stanislavski techniques ever created. Its intent is nothing less than to take the actor to a consistency of artistry on a transpersonal level (beyond self)."
Lee K. Korf
Educational Theatre News

"Ahead of its time. A manual that incorporates consciousness theory and brain research findings."
Marilyn Ferguson
Author, The Aquarian Conspiracy

"...profound, solid and a new departure."
Sidney Lanier
Founder
The American Place Theatre

Published by MANDERINO BOOKS
P.O. Box 27758, Los Angeles, CA 90027

ISBN 0-9601194-5-0